State Postsecondary
Education Research

Stylus Higher Education Policy Series

Higher education is facing fundamental questions about financing, affordability, access, quality, outcomes, and diversity. College and university administrators, as well as state and federal policymakers, need reliable data, effective interpretation of research, innovative ideas, and cogent analysis to guide them in the critical decisions they will be facing in the near and long term.

The series aims to bring together the nation's most respected researchers, scholars, and policy analysts to inform the debate on these issues and help shape future policy.

Series Editor: Donald E. Heller, associate professor and senior research associate at the Center for the Study of Higher Education, The Pennsylvania State University.

Submissions: The editor and publisher welcome proposals for volumes in the series. E-mail dheller@psu.edu

State Postsecondary Education Research

New Methods to Inform Policy and Practice

Edited by
Kathleen M. Shaw and Donald E. Heller

STERLING, VIRGINIA

COPYRIGHT © 2007 BY STYLUS PUBLISHING, LLC.

Published by Stylus Publishing, LLC
22883 Quicksilver Drive
Sterling, Virginia 20166-2102

Library of Congress Cataloging-in-Publication-Data
State postsecondary education research : new methods to inform policy and practice / edited by Kathleen M. Shaw and Donald E. Heller.—1st ed.
     p. cm.— (Stylus higher education policy series)
   Includes bibliographical references and index.
   ISBN-13: 978-1-57922-211-6 (pbk. : alk. paper)
   ISBN-10: 1-57922-211-0 (pbk. : alk. paper)
   1. Higher education and state—United States. 2. Higher education and state—Research—United States.
I. Shaw, Kathleen M. II. Heller, Donald E.
LC173.S73 2007
378.007′2—dc22

2006026462

ISBN: 1-57922-211-0 (paper) /
13-digit ISBN: 978-1-57922-211-6

Printed in Canada

All first editions printed on acid free paper that meets the American National Standards Institute Z39-48 Standard.

Bulk Purchases

Quantity discounts are available for use in workshops and for staff development.
Call 1-800-232-0223

First Edition, 2007

10 9 8 7 6 5 4 3 2 1

Acknowledgments

The idea for this book was developed following a symposium held at the 2004 annual conference of the Association for the Study of Higher Education in Kansas City. The editors and a number of the authors participated in a panel on the challenges of conducting state-level policy research, a spirited discussion that raised issues of interest to many researchers and policymakers, based on the audience's reaction.

Following the conference we spoke with some of the participants in the symposium, as well as other researchers who we knew were working on state-level higher education policy research, about the possibility of contributing to this book. We received an enthusiastic response, so our first note of gratitude goes to the authors who took the time to prepare chapters for this volume. Working on book projects is not always the highest priority for academic or policy researchers, so we appreciate the time and effort that they all put into their chapters as they worked with us through what were often multiple editing cycles. Without their efforts, this book would never have come to fruition.

Without a publishing and production team, no book would ever see the light of day. This is certainly true of our volume, which benefited from the work of a number of people at Stylus Publishing, LLC. John von Knorring, president of Stylus, originated the Higher-Education Policy Series and was an enthusiastic supporter of this volume as a part of that series from the time we first proposed it to him. The book was shepherded through the production process at Stylus by Judy Coughlin and benefited from the copyediting expertise of Linda Carlson. We greatly appreciate the efforts of the entire Stylus team.

Last, we would be remiss if we did not thank our spouses, John Noakes and Anne Simon. Both have been extremely supportive of our academic careers, at times even more so than could be expected of any reasonable person. Without that support, this book—and so much more of our scholarly work—would not be possible.

Kathleen M. Shaw
Donald E. Heller
August 2006

Contents

The Challenges of Comparative State-Level Higher Education Policy Research

Donald E. Heller

The United States is distinct from most other countries in that it has very limited federal oversight and control of postsecondary education. Whereas most other developed countries maintain some form of federal ministry of education that has responsibility for all levels, including post-secondary education, the U.S. Constitution prescribes no role for the federal government in higher education. The word *education*, in fact, never appears in the Constitution or its amendments. By virtue of the 10th amendment, which states, "The powers not delegated to the United States by the Constitution, nor prohibited by it to the States, are reserved to the States respectively, or to the people," authority over all levels of education is delegated to the states (U.S. Government Printing Office, 2006).

The federal government does have a role in postsecondary education, but that role is primarily one of providing funding for various aspects. This role has extended for more than a century and a half, beginning with the Morrill Act of 1862, which provided the first large-scale financial support from the federal government for colleges (Brubacher & Rudy, 1976; Rudolph, 1990). Subsequent federal legislation, including the second Morrill Act (1892), the G.I. Bill (1944), the National Defense Education Act (1958), and the Higher Education Act of 1965 (and its subsequent reauthorizations), all provided funding for colleges and/or for their students. In addition, numerous federal agencies provide research funds to U.S. colleges and universities.

Although the federal government has long had a role in funding higher education, authority for operating the nation's postsecondary institutions has been the responsibility of states and private entities. Of the nation's approximately 4,200 degree-granting postsecondary institutions that participate in the federal government's Title IV student aid programs, approximately 40 percent are controlled and operated by the 50 states and the District of Columbia (National Center for Education Statistics, 2006).[1] These institutions enrolled 74 percent of the nation's 17.3 million college students in 2003. Because of the large state role in postsecondary education, understanding how state policy affects these 1,700 institutions and their 13 million students is an important task for researchers.[2] The states provide a natural experiment for researchers, where individual state policies can be examined to determine their impact on the effectiveness, efficiency, and quality of colleges and universities.

Higher education in the states differs along a number of dimensions. Some states, such as many of those in the northeastern region of the United States, have a relatively large number of private colleges and universities. Many of these states are characterized by public institutions with higher tuition rates and state-funded scholarship programs that provide large amounts of assistance to students attending public and private postsecondary institutions. In contrast, other regions of the country, such as the West, have many fewer private colleges, and the public institutions dominate both in terms of student enrollment and in setting the agenda for postsecondary education policy.

States also differ in the governance and control of the postsecondary system. Some states (Georgia is one example) have fairly strong statewide control of the public institutions, where a centralized governing board has responsibility for planning, governance, and oversight of the entire postsecondary system.[3] Other states (such as Michigan and Pennsylvania) have relatively little state oversight of the postsecondary system and grant a great deal of autonomy to individual institutions and their governing boards.

States also differ on their financial support for higher education. An annual survey conducted by the Center for the Study of Education Policy (2006) at Illinois State University reports the amount states spend per capita on higher education. In fiscal year 2006, these ranged from a high of $434 per person in Wyoming, to a low of $89 in New Hampshire. Similarly, there is wide variation in how much money states appropriate for their state-run student aid programs. In fiscal year 2005, this ranged from a low of zero in Alaska and South Dakota, the only two states without a state aid program, to a high of $58 per capita in South Carolina (National Association of State Student Grant & Aid Programs, 2006).

Because of this great variation among the states in terms of the structure, governance, and funding of higher education, researchers are provided with the opportunity to conduct studies that exploit these differences in order to examine a variety of outcomes. They can ask questions regarding the efficiency and effectiveness of public systems of higher education and whether differences across the states lead to different outcomes, and they can also conduct comparative analyses that examine whether, and how, the development or implementation of higher education policy differs across states.

This is a critically important time for the field of higher education to be engaged in examining policy via cross-state comparative analyses. Momentous court, legislative, and policy developments with clear and important implications for state-level higher education policy are emerging at a rapid rate. These include recent affirmative action rulings, such as the Supreme Court's 2003 decisions in the University of Michigan cases (*Gratz v. Bollinger*, 2003; *Grutter v. Bollinger*, 2003), as well as the current debates over reauthorization of the Higher Education Act. Recent passage and reauthorization of major federal initiatives such as welfare reform (the Personal Responsibility and Work Opportunity Reconciliation Act) and the Workforce Investment Act have also had important implications for states and their higher education institutions, because they have an effect on the number and flow of low-income students into the postsecondary sector. Over the past two decades the states have emerged as prolific postsecondary education policy innovators, developing new policies in the areas of student financing (e.g., merit scholarship programs, college savings programs, and prepaid tuition programs), institutional accountability (e.g., performance-funding and budgeting regimes), and student access (e.g., "10-percent Plans" etc.) (Heller, 2002; Zumeta, 1998).

Moreover, in recent years political scientists have rediscovered the American states as a unit of analysis. Given their substantial variation along key social, cultural, and institutional dimensions, the American states provide a unique venue in which to test propositions about a wide range of political behavior, including policy adoption dynamics. However, both the enactment of policy changes and response to them is not uniform across states. Thus, if we are to understand the antecedents, implementation, and impact of major policy, the state is a critically important unit of analysis. Indeed, from a comparative standpoint, the states represent a natural laboratory for testing theory and hypotheses about policies and the institutions in which those policies are created.

On a more practical level, the current period is a particularly opportune one in which to study policy from a comparative-state perspective. The boom and bust fiscal cycles of the 1990s and first decade of the twenty-first century created dynamic budget challenges for the states. Devolution trends reaffirmed the states' preeminent role, vis-à-vis that of the federal government, in some policy arenas (e.g., welfare reform and systemic K–12 education reform). Important changes within state governments (e.g., movements to professionalize legislatures, term-limit legislators, and "reinvent" government) have made cross-state policy analysis increasingly important as we strive to understand the effects of these policies on higher education institutions and their students (Gray, 1994; Osborne & Gaebler, 1992; Rosenthal, 1998). Analytically, the development of new research techniques and the reemergence of some older ones have provided scholars leverage in analyzing higher education policies both across states and over time. For example, pooled cross-sectional time-series analytic techniques and event history analysis, now widespread within the disciplines of economics and political science, respectively, have helped shift the unit of analysis from the *state* to the *state-year*, thus expanding greatly both the statistical power of the models being tested and the data-demands of those models (Berry & Berry, 1990, 1992; Gray, 1994; Mintrom, 1997). Advances in quantitative methodology have been met by important developments in qualitative research methodology as well. For example, both case studies and elite interviewing have emerged in the disciplines as important strategies for conducting comparative-state research on policies and the policy behavior of governments (King, Keohane, & Verba, 1994).

This volume provides an in-depth examination of both the challenges and the opportunities inherent in conducting cross-state higher education policy research. The primary focus of the book is not on the results of the authors' individual research projects; rather, the volume uses these research projects as tools with which to examine the array of methodological, theoretical, analytical, and political challenges inherent in conducting comparative state-level policy research. The book brings together researchers with a wide array of experience in the substantive questions regarding state policy as well as in the use of tools with which they conduct those studies.

Following this introduction, Michael K. McLendon and James C. Hearn examine the conceptual, methodological, and practical opportunities and challenges associated with collecting political-system data and integrating those data into comparative analysis of postsecondary policy adoption by the states. The authors analyze the role of states serving as multiple laboratories of policy experimentation, where new ideas and approaches to solving policy problems continually evolve. The states also represent fifty units of analysis, whose constrained variance along demographic, economic, political, and institutional dimensions permits the testing of propositions about governments and the policies they adopt.

McLendon and Hearn's chapter draws on two sources of insight: a review of the policy innovation and diffusion literatures of political science and organizational theory and their own recent, major data collection project, which culminated in a unique dataset of state-level indicators that they are now using in various analyses. First, they open with a review of the policy innovation and diffusion literatures (e.g., Berry & Berry, 1992; Mintrom, 1997; Walker, 1969) that aim toward the development of a new conceptual framework for postsecondary researchers. Specifically, the framework views the 50 states both as individual policy actors and as agents of potential mutual influence within a larger social system (American federalism). It holds that states adopt the policies they do in part because of their internal social, demographic, economic, and political characteristics and in part because of their ability to influence one another's behavior. From this literature review emerges a list of state-level political indicators common to the political science literature but rarely used by postsecondary researchers.

Second, drawing on their own recent experiences, the authors discuss the opportunities and challenges researchers face in collecting and using these political data in analysis of postsecondary policy adoption both across states and over time. They examine important questions these data raise about theoretical relevancy, sample selection, variable measurement, and analytic approach. The chapter provides postsecondary researchers with 1) a conceptual rationale for including political-system data in comparative-state analysis, 2) new sources of information regarding potential study variables and data sources, and 3) improved understanding of the design issues involved in use of these data.

The next chapter describes a study conducted by Kathleen M. Shaw and Thomas Bailey that examined a project geared at improving education in the public two-year sector. The project, entitled the "Bridges to Opportunity" Initiative, was funded by the Ford Foundation. It seeks to promote state policies that enhance the capacity of community college systems in six states to improve the educational and economic opportunities for low-income adults on a large scale. The Bridges initiative uses a theory of change that focuses on the engagement of a wide variety of constituencies with a stake in increasing access to education for low-income adults (Colburn & Driver, 2003).

A team of researchers based at the Community College Research Center at Teachers College, Columbia University, conducted a series of multiyear case studies in each of the six states in order to examine the implementation of the Bridges to Opportunity Initiative and to examine as well the salience of the theory of change that was developed by the Ford Foundation and serves as a basis to the initiative. As members of the research team that conducted the study, Shaw and Bailey begin by introducing the theoretical model and defining its elements in operational terms. They then discuss the degree to which a wide range of factors, including the structure of the higher education governance system, the economic and political environment of the state, and historical antecedents, present both analytical and theoretical challenges in conducting comparative analyses of the states and their progress on implementing the Bridges to Opportunity Initiative.

Following the chapter by Shaw and Bailey, Jennifer A. Delaney and William R. Doyle examine the role that higher education plays in state budgets. Considering a theory presented by Harold Hovey (Hovey, 1999), the authors use an empirical analysis to consider whether changes in higher education funding fall in line with a "balance wheel" framework in state budgets. The balance wheel framework has two parts. First, when a state's revenues are low, higher education is an attractive option for heavy cuts, because it has the ability to collect fees for its services (an ability lacking from most other major state spending categories such as K–12 education, Medicaid, or corrections). Second, when state revenues are high, higher education is a politically attractive area in which to spend money.

The authors apply Hovey's balance wheel theory to analyze whether the magnitude of the change in higher education funding has a greater absolute value than changes in all other categories, in both good times and bad. In other words, they ask the question: As changes in spending for all other categories decline, does the change in higher education spending decline even further? As changes in spending for all other categories increase, does the change in spending for higher education increase even faster? The critical aspect of Hovey's theory that the authors test is the nonlinear relationship between higher education and other budget categories, which would confirm Hovey's balance wheel model.

At a broad level, Delaney and Doyle's findings about higher education are important because they add to our general knowledge about state budgets and the budget decision-making process. In addition, the authors' study offers insight into the relationship between higher education and other state budget categories. It also provides a model for understanding higher education expenditures in state budgets.

Next, Sara Goldrick-Rab and Kathleen M. Shaw look at how an examination of the process of policy implementation is becoming an increasingly important component of policy research. Traditional policy analyses tend to ignore how shifts in ideas lead to changes in public policy or assume that the relationship between ideas and policy implementation is relatively straightforward. Yet increasingly, we know that the ideology and political beliefs that underlie the development of public policy are often not shared among those who are responsible for implementing it. Powerful forces such as cultural and institutional belief systems at both the macro and micro levels structure organizational systems and dictate to a large extent the degree to which policy developed at a federal or state level is enacted at the local level. Thus, a wide array of data collected from multiple sources and levels of analysis is necessary to develop a thorough understanding of the policy implementation process.

Goldrick-Rab and Shaw's chapter focuses on the difficulties inherent in developing a database that is sufficient to arrive at an in-depth understanding of policy implementation across six diverse states. The presentation is based on a four-year project, funded by multiple foundations, to examine how two pieces of federal legislation directly affecting higher education—welfare reform and the Workforce Investment Act—have been implemented at the state and local levels. Using an array of quantitative and qualitative data, the authors provide examples of both the challenges and the promise of conducting cross-state comparisons of policy implementation. They focus in particular on the difficulties in tracking the development and dissemination of the ideas that support the policies at the federal level and documenting how such ideas are either enacted or resisted at the state and local levels.

In the next chapter, William R. Doyle builds on the experience of the project team that produced *Measuring Up: The National Report Card on Higher Education* (National Center for Public Policy and Higher Education, 2004). *Measuring Up* provides a framework for policymakers who are interested in how well the system of higher education in their state meets the needs of the public, and it evaluates states based on how well they are expanding both opportunity and achievement at the postsecondary level.

Doyle describes the work of the Resources and Performance Project, which is designed to add to *Measuring Up* by creating a similarly responsible comparison among the levels of resources that are available for higher education in the 50 states. There are multiple challenges to accurately measuring how much funding is available. The major conceptual challenge in creating indicators of resources for all 50 states involves differences in utilization of the various sectors of higher education. The major methodological issue for the resources and performance project involves the use of Integrated Postsecondary Education Data Systems (IPEDS) finance data. The IPEDS data underwent a dramatic change in the 1990s as private institutions began implementing the Financial Accounting Standards Board standards for reporting data. Public institutions are currently implementing similar changes as they change over to Government Accounting Standard Board standards. This change means institutions report data from an institution as a whole perspective, as opposed to the old accounting method, which segregated revenues and expenditures into separate reporting categories. Another challenge involves the comparison of data reported under different standards over time.

Doyle's chapter details how the Resources and Performance Project addressed these challenges in order to create a useful comparison of funding for higher education in the 50 states. He also provides guidance for researchers conducting similar cross-state comparative studies who face challenges in compatibility of data across both states and time.

The final chapter of this volume, by Karen Paulson, describes a collaborative effort of three well-respected higher education policy organizations—the Education Commission of the States, the National Center for Public Policy and Higher Education, and the National Center for Higher Education Management Systems. The project's purpose was to test an approach to developing and implementing a state public agenda for higher education.

Paulson's chapter focuses on methodological problems that arise when conducting activities with states pursuing the development of a public agenda for higher education systems and institutions. She describes these problems and how the project overcame them in order to help the states develop an agenda for higher education. The chapter presents some of the lessons learned by the project team and its constituent organizations while working with these states, and it provides guidance for others who work across states with data, policies, and institutions in the postsecondary-education domain.

The chapters in this volume make an important contribution to the research on the intersection of state policy and postsecondary education in the United States. The methodological and substantive issues addressed by the authors demonstrate the opportunities provided by learning from research in other policy domains and applying these tools and techniques to higher education. There are still many challenges left for higher education researchers, policymakers, and others before we have a more complete understanding of how state policy decisions can help—or harm—colleges, universities, and their students. This book should help pave the way toward that understanding.

Notes

1. Institutions participating in the federal Title IV aid programs, which include grant, loan, and work-study assistance, must be accredited by a body approved by the U.S. Department of Education. The only postsecondary institutions controlled and operated by the federal government are the four military academies.

2. States also affect students in private institutions, through funding for student aid and institutional appropriations for private institutions, as well as through laws on licensing of private institutions.
3. See Education Commission of the States (2002) for a taxonomy of the postsecondary governance structures employed by the 50 states.

References

Berry, F. S., & Berry, W. D. (1990). State lottery adoptions as policy innovations: An event history analysis. *American Political Science Review, 84*, 395–416.

Berry, F. S., & Berry, W. D. (1992). Tax innovation in the states: Capitalizing on political opportunity. *American Journal of Political Science, 34*, 715–742.

Brubacher, J. S., & Rudy, W. (1976). *Higher education in transition: A history of American colleges and universities, 1636–1976* (Third ed.). New York: Harper & Row.

Center for the Study of Education Policy. (2006). *Appropriations of state tax funds for operating expenses of higher education.* Retrieved May 6, 2006, from www.coe.ilstu.edu/grapevine/

Colburn, J., & Driver, C. (2003). Stakeholder engagement model, unpublished document. New York: Ford Foundation.

Education Commission of the States. (2002). *Postsecondary governance structures database.* Denver, CO: Author.

Gratz v. Bollinger, 123 2411 (S. Ct. 2003).

Gray, V. (1994). Competition, emulation, and policy innovation. In Dodd, L. & Jillson, C. (Eds.), *New perspectives on American politics.* Washington, DC: CQ Press.

Grutter v. Bollinger, 124 35 (S. Ct. 2003).

Heller, D. E. (2002). The policy shift in state financial aid programs. In Smart, J. C. (Ed.), *Higher education: Handbook of theory and research* (Vol. 17, pp. 221–261). New York: Agathon Press.

Hovey, H. A. (1999). *State spending for higher education in the next decade: The battle to sustain current support.* San Jose, CA: National Center for Public Policy and Higher Education.

King, G., Keohane, R. O., & Verba, S. (1994). *Designing social inquiry: Scientific inference in qualitative research.* Princeton, NJ: Princeton University Press.

Mintrom, M. (1997). Policy entrepreneurs and the diffusion of innovation. *American Journal of Political Science, 41*, 738–770.

National Association of State Student Grant & Aid Programs. (2006). *NASSGAP 36th annual survey report on state-sponsored student financial aid 2004–2005 academic year.* Springfield: Illinois Student Assistance Commission.

National Center for Education Statistics. (2006). *2005 Digest of Education Statistics.* Retrieved May 25, 2006, from http://nces.ed.gov/programs/digest/d05_tf.asp

National Center for Public Policy and Higher Education. (2004). *Measuring up 2004: The national report card on higher education.* San Jose, CA: Author.

Osborne, D., & Gaebler, T. (1992). *Reinventing government*. Reading, MA: Addison-Wesley.

Rosenthal, A. (1998). *The decline of representative democracy*. Washington, DC: CQ Press.

Rudolph, F. (1990). *The American college and university: A history* (1990 ed.). Athens: University of Georgia Press.

U.S. Government Printing Office. (2006). *Constitution of the United States: Browse, 2002 edition & supplements*. Retrieved May 25, 2006, from www .gpoaccess.gov/constitution/browse2002.html

Walker, J. L. (1969). The diffusion of innovations among the American states. *Political Science Review, 63*(3), 880–899.

Zumeta, W. (1998). Public university accountability to the state in the late twentieth century: Time for a rethinking? *Policy Studies Review, 15*(4), 5–22.

CHAPTER 1

Incorporating Political Indicators into Comparative State Study of Higher Education Policy

Michael K. McLendon and James C. Hearn

Traditionally, the state policy literature on higher education has exhibited a major blind spot: Research has focused nearly exclusively on policy *effects*, ignoring consideration of the *determinants* of state policy for higher education. A substantial empirical literature exists on the effects of state policies on students (e.g., impacts of financial aid regimes on college attendance), on campuses (e.g., consequences of state regulation for campus quality), and on society more broadly (e.g., the contribution of higher education to economic development). Yet, scholars have studied factors associated with interstate variation in public policy for higher education far less frequently. Thus, although the current era has witnessed dynamic policy changes for higher education,[1] our understanding of the forces that have led states to reform and adopt new policies remains rudimentary.

The ignoring of *political* determinants of policy is especially troubling. Until very recently, students of higher education largely overlooked political science as a framework for organizing state policy research. This omission seems vexing on a number of levels. First, researchers seeking to explain the policy choices state governments make for higher education should surely account for the governmental contexts in which those choices are made, in much the same way as studies of the decisions of students (e.g., what college to attend, whether to drop out, etc.) or of colleges and universities (e.g., tuition setting) typically seek to account for key attributes of the individual or the institution of interest. One important context conditioning the policy choices of state governments is the *political* context, which is defined by the constellation of state political institutions, actors, and processes within which governmental behavior is nested. Any serious attempt to explain governmental behavior requires, we believe, some systematic attention to be paid to the potential policy impacts of these state political forces.

Second, failure to account for the political context in which policies arise is a missed opportunity, since the American states provide one of the world's most attractive venues in which to comparatively study the formation of public policy. Thus, across Alabama, California, Nebraska, Rhode Island, and beyond, the 50 states represent a system of constrained variation along key demographic, economic, organizational, *and political* dimensions that makes possible rigorous comparisons.[2] From a comparative standpoint, in fact, the states represent an almost ideal "natural laboratory" for testing hypotheses about policies and the contextual conditions that produce them (Dye, 1990). Accordingly, political scientists in recent decades have "rediscovered" the American states as an arena in which to study policy, refining their theoretical and methodological approaches so as to better leverage across-state comparisons (Brace & Jewett, 1995; Moncrief, Thompson, & Cassie, 1996; Squire & Hamm, 2005). Contemporary researchers on state policy for higher education thus stand to benefit from two broader developments: a realization among policy scholars that the American states provide a unique opportunity for comparative analysis and the advent of new conceptualizations, measures, and analytic techniques with which to pursue comparative political analyses of state policy.

Our aim in this chapter is to build on these recent developments by providing a framework for, and describing some challenges attendant to, incorporating select indicators of political systems into comparative-state research on higher education policy. To help guide researchers, we first develop a conceptual framework for studying policy adoption and change in the American states. Our framework views the 50 states both as individual policy actors and as agents of potential mutual influence within a larger social system. It holds that states adopt the policies they do in part because of their internal demographic, economic, and political characteristics and in part because of their ability to influence one another's behavior. In this discussion, we identify key political indicators and data sources commonly found in the comparative state policy literature but rarely incorporated into higher education research. We then discuss five challenges that researchers would face in integrating these data into their work.

A Framework for Studying and Incorporating Political Indicators into Comparative-State Study of Higher Education Policy

Although research on state policy innovation and diffusion can be traced to classic work in the fields of rural sociology, organizational theory, and communication studies (Katz, Levin, & Hamilton, 1963; Mohr, 1969; Rogers, 1962), much of the systematic scholarship in recent decades has been undertaken by political scientists, who have developed conceptual and analytical tools of increasing sophistication with which to examine governmental behavior in the states. The policy innovation and diffusion perspective holds that states adopt the policies they do partly because of the demographic, socioeconomic, and political features arising within them individually (i.e., innovation) and partly because of their ability to influence one another's behavior (i.e., diffusion).[3] Walker's (1969) early investigation was the first to conceptually integrate both sets of considerations—intrastate and interstate. His factor analysis of the adoption of policies over time indicated that certain characteristics internal to states influenced patterns of policy adoption, but that states also seemed to emulate the behavior of their neighbors, thus leading over time to the spread of policies along regional lines.

The more recent work of Berry and Berry (1990) produced conceptual and analytical refinements through their pioneering use of *event history analysis*. They found that states adopted new lotteries and taxes because of a combination of within-state and across-state forces. Numerous studies in recent years have built on the Berrys's research, examining school choice initiatives, consumer protection laws, health insurance reforms, and abortion and death-penalty statutes (Hays, 1996; Mintrom, 1997; Mintrom & Vergari, 1998; Mooney & Lee, 1999; Stream, 1999). Higher education researchers also have begun incorporating this framework into their studies (Doyle, 2005; Hearn & Griswold, 1994; McLendon, Hearn, & Deaton, 2006; McLendon, Heller, & Young, 2005).

Building on this scholarship, we propose a framework for comparative analysis that conceptualizes state policy outcomes for higher education as being a function of many of the same factors that research has shown to influence policy in other arenas. Our framework includes policy influences arising both within states (e.g., higher education organization patterns, economic conditions, and a host of political factors, including political culture and ideology, legislative design, partisanship, gubernatorial influence, and interest group climates) and between and among them (i.e., diffusion pressures).

We issue two caveats, however. First, we would not characterize our framework as approximating a unified theory of governmental behavior. Instead, we propose a set of broad categories, variables, and indicators that are already staples of research in political science, but whose inclusion into the higher education literature would help to stimulate scholarship and capitalize on the unique contextual and comparative analytical advantages that attend state-level research. Second, given the space limitations of the chapter, our topical coverage is highly abridged; we focus on select variables, indicators, and data sources that we believe hold promise in building models capable of predicting and explaining policy outcomes for higher education across state settings.

Higher Education Demography, Organization, and Governance

Although most of the prospective influences on higher education policy that we discuss in this section focus on the broader political economies of states, a substantial body of empirical research supports the view that conditions and factors native to higher education might influence state policy outcomes. For example, certain demographic and postsecondary enrollment patterns (e.g., nonresident enrollments, state population share by age, etc.) and organization-ecologic features of higher education (e.g., the mix of two- and four-year and public and private institutions) have been shown to influence variation in public-sector tuition levels and student financing policies (e.g., Hearn, Griswold, & Marine, 1996; Heller, 1997; Rizzo & Ehrenberg, 2004; Zumeta, 1996). Data on these indicators are readily available to researchers via the Integrated Postsecondary Education Data Systems (IPEDS) and similar sources and have been routinely incorporated into previous studies of higher education policy.

A growing body of empirical research also points to connections between postsecondary governance arrangements and policy outcomes for higher education at both the state and campus levels. Indeed, research continues to accumulate in favor of the view that various aspects of the governance climate for higher education, including the overall statewide approach to governance (e.g., coordinating or governing board), the number of separately governed boards in a state, and the mode of trustee selection (i.e., elected versus appointed), could help condition the higher education policies states adopt (Hearn & Griswold, 1994; Hearn et al., 1996; Knott & Payne, 2004; Lowry, 2001; McLendon, 2003; McLendon et al., 2006; Zumeta, 1996). Editions of McGuinness's (e.g., 1997) widely cited handbook on postsecondary governance structures are the leading sources of comparative data on these and other governance dimensions.

Ideally, an integrative model seeking to account for the determinants of state policy for higher education across the 50 states would include appropriate controls for the governance landscapes of state postsecondary systems, as well as the demographic and organizational features previously noted.

Socioeconomic Climates

One long-standing debate in the comparative-state policy literature involves the relative importance of economic and political factors as determinants of governmental behavior. One of the early, robust findings of research was that socioeconomic development patterns seemed to account for much of the interstate variation in public policy. In such classic studies as those by Dawson and Robinson (1963) and Dye (1966), researchers identified strong, positive relationships between levels of educational attainment, wealth, and industrialization and public expenditures. In some instances, evidence seemed also to point to a connection between higher levels of socioeconomic development and state adoption of *new* policies (e.g., Walker, 1969). Although much of the research of the past 20 years has dispelled the myth of economic determinism (e.g., Jacoby & Schneider, 2001), our read of the literature leads us to believe that both distal and proximal[4] socioeconomic conditions are likely to play some role in shaping the policy choices states make for higher education.

Political Culture and Ideology

Our first category of systemic *political* influences emphasizes variation across states in political culture and ideology. A staple of the comparative policy literature since Elazar's influential work in the 1960s (Elazar, 1966), *political culture* refers to contrasting collective conceptions of U.S. political order that might shape both the structure of state political systems and the policies arising within those systems (Gray, 2003). Elazar argued that early migration and settlement patterns produced several regional political subcultures in the United States, each producing a distinctive vision regarding the role of government in public life.[5] Although interest in Elazar's cultural theory of state politics and policy has waned, his ideas remain intuitively appealing. Additionally, some subsequent empirical work has demonstrated connections between political culture, as defined by Elazar, and the policies states adopt (Erikson, Wright, & McIver, 1993; Fitzpatrick & Hero, 1988; Sharkansky, 1969).

Numerous other scholars have attempted to map the *political ideologies* of states' citizenries and government officials. Broadly speaking, political ideology can be understood as a coherent and consistent set of orientations or attitudes toward politics. Berry, Ringquist, Fording, and Hanson (1998) defined *citizen ideology* as the mean position on a liberal-conservative continuum of the electorate in a state and state *government ideology* as the mean position of the elected public officials in a state. In one creative undertaking, Erikson, Wright, and McIver (1993) pooled the results of more than 100 national telephone surveys from 1976 to 1988 to obtain measures of *ideology* by state, concluding (via multivariate analysis) both that the political attitudes of Americans vary according to where in the United States they live and that these attitudes appear to be linked with certain state policy choices. One criticism of the measures developed by Erikson et al. (1993) is that these cross-sectional snapshots ignore significant changes in ideological orientations over time, thus leading to outdated measures (Berry at al., 1998, p. 328). In an effort to address these limitations, Berry et al. (1998) created what are perhaps now the leading indicators of state political, developing multiple, and longitudinal measures of roll-call voting, outcomes of congressional elections, partisan balance of state legislatures, and party of the governor. Using these measures, a number of studies have subsequently demonstrated strong empirical connections between the ideological propensities of citizens and politicians and certain policy outcomes in the states, notably in the areas of welfare and corrections (e.g., Soss, Schram, Vartanian, & O'Brien, 2001; Yates & Fording, 2005).

Political culture and ideology is one area in which higher education researchers have made limited use of existing indicators (e.g., Doyle, McLendon, & Hearn, 2005; Hossler, Lund, Ramin, Westfall, & Irish, 1997; Nicholson-Crotty & Meier, 2003; Volkwein, 1987).[6] Yet, most researchers who have pursued political ideology and culture have done so using cross-sectional measures, a problematical practice, given the dynamic nature of public opinion. Fortunately, the index developed by Berry et al., which assigns ideology scores for all states for all years between 1960 and 2002, has demonstrated high levels of validity and reliability and is available publicly (Berry et al., 2004).

Legislative Organization and Membership

The second category of political influences involves certain structural features of state legislatures that might influence policy outcomes. Through constitutional and statutory provisions, and by tradition, state legislative bodies have been designed in ways that are broadly similar in form, but that vary by degree along important dimensions. For example, *legislative professionalism* refers to organizational properties of legislatures that are capable of shaping policy. State legislative assemblies that meet in extended session, pay their members well, and provide ample staff resources (i.e., ones like the U.S. Congress) are considered professionalized. Legislatures with session lengths of brief duration, low pay for members, and few staff are deemed as nonprofessional "citizen legislatures" (Squire, 2000). The variation that exists in the professionalism of legislatures holds implications for policy. Professionalism can directly influence policy in that greater analytical capacity (e.g., more staff) tends to produce higher volumes of legislation. Professionalism also can influence policy indirectly in that professionalized settings tend to attract better-educated legislators, ones who might be more inclined toward new policy approaches (e.g., Barrilleaux, Holbrook, & Langer, 2002; Squire, 1992, 2000).

State legislatures vary organizationally in other respects, including the powers accorded leadership, the means of allocating committee assignments, the terms permitted officeholders, and the perquisites of incumbency that shape the goals, strategies, and behaviors of members. All of these factors might play *some* role in shaping policy differences among states, although the strength of evidence varies across settings and issues (Carey, Niemi, & Powell, 2001; Jewell & Whicker, 1994; Oppenheimer, 1985; Squire & Hamm, 2005). Research also indicates that certain *demographic* differences among legislatures can hold important implications for policy development (Moncrief et al., 1996; Squire & Hamm, 2005). For example, women and men tend to perceive issues differently, and these differences influence the amount and the types of legislation passed in the states, including legislation relating to education (Thomas, 1991).

Higher education researchers have paid somewhat greater attention to legislatures than they have to other aspects of state political systems. One of the earliest across-state studies was Eulau and Quinley's (1970) investigation of legislative norms toward higher education. These analysts interviewed nearly 100 legislators, identifying four principal political norms that seemed to govern state policy for higher education in the 1960s. Since the work of Eulau and Quinley, most research has examined the impact of certain institutional features of legislatures on higher education policy. For example, Volkwein's (1987) cross-sectional analysis found correlational evidence of relationships between well-staffed legislatures and levels of state regulation of higher education. Recent *longitudinal* studies, however, point curiously to a set of bifurcated findings. On the one hand, studies examining the impact of state political climates on *campus-level* policy have tended to confirm the predictive value of certain legislative attributes. Nicholson-Crotty and Meier (2003) found legislative professionalism associated with higher tuition levels. Hicklin and Hawes's (2004) hierarchical linear model of 500 universities over an 11-year period found that increased representation of African Americans and Latinos in legislatures positively influenced levels of minority student enrollment at public universities. Yet, studies of the determinants of *state-level* policies for higher education often have failed to find connections between legislative organization or membership and state policy outcomes (Doyle, 2005; Doyle et al., 2005; McLendon et al., 2006; McLendon, Heller, & Young, 2005).

This divergence in findings suggests the desirability of further research aimed toward identifying the conditions under which certain legislative attributes help determine higher education policy outcomes. A number of publicly available measures of legislative professionalism exist to aid in such work. The most widely used measure of professionalism is Squire's index (1992, 2000), which assigns states values ranging from 0 to 1. His measure relies on an index of Congress's member pay, average days in session, and mean staff per member as a baseline against which to compare an index composed of those same attributes of state legislative bodies. One drawback of the Squire index is that it is updated only periodically and, thus, although published versions of the index are capable of capturing general trends in legislative capacity, they cannot account for short-term changes in legislatures that might impact policy in a given year. The individual, state-level elements comprising Squire's index, however, can be found in annual volumes of the Council of State Government's *Book of the States* (e.g., Council, 2004), thus researchers could create similar metrics conveying the position of the states relative to one another. Although there are no data sets publicly available containing comprehensive, longitudinal information on most of the demographic indicators that we have discussed, select data on women legislators can be obtained publicly through the Center for American Women and Politics (2005) and data on black legislators can be purchased from the Joint Center for Political and Economic Studies (2005).

Gubernatorial Influence

The separation-of-powers system that characterizes American state government also ensures governors a prominent role in shaping public policy. Although governors everywhere exert considerable sway, the precise extent of their influence over public policy processes and outcomes varies from one state to the next, depending in part on the *governors' institutional and personal powers* (Beyle, 2003). In some states, for example, governors wield stronger influence over policy through the line-item veto, broad appointment powers, and robust tenure potential. Elsewhere, governors hold fewer formal instruments of policy control, thus limiting their influence (Barrilleaux & Bernick, 2003; Beyle, 2003; Dometrius, 1987). The policy influence of governors overall, however, appears to rest on a

dynamic variable

combination of contextual factors, including the professionalism of the legislature, the strength of political parties, and the strength of the economy (Dilger, Krause, & Moffett, 1995).

Only a handful of published studies have sought to account systematically for the influence of governors on higher education policy (e.g., Lowry, 2001; Nicholson-Crotty & Meier, 2003; McLendon, Deaton, & Hearn, 2005; McLendon et al., 2006; Volkwein, 1987). Lowry's (2001) approach, linking governors, bureaucracies, and the behaviors of public universities, warrants extended discussion.[7] Drawing on principal-agent theory, Lowry conceptualized state governance structures for higher education as, in effect, systems of political representation, because the different institutional arrangements "affect the ability of different actors to influence decisions" (p. 846). Lowry reasoned that *regulatory coordinating boards*[8] essentially are extensions of governors' capacity to supervise, because they appoint board members. Consequently, regulatory boards should behave in a manner generally consistent with the preferences of governors (and voters), leading to lower tuition levels. By contrast, governance structures lacking such direct political oversight should tend to institutionalize the preferences of faculty and administrators, resulting in higher tuition levels. Estimating a series of models using data on 407 public universities for a single year, 1995, Lowry found that universities located in states with regulatory boards in fact charged significantly lower prices.

Although Lowry's work illustrates one creative approach to studying gubernatorial influence in higher education,[9] the conventional measures of gubernatorial power are those indices created originally by Schlesinger (1965) and subsequently revised and periodically updated by Beyle (2003).[10] Beyle's institutional-powers variable is a metric combining scores on six individual indices: governor's tenure potential, appointment power, budget power, veto power, extent to which the governor's party also control the legislature, and whether the state provides for separately elected executive branch officials. The personal-power variable also is a metric combining separate measures for electoral mandate, ambition ladder, personal future, personal style, and job performance rating. Beyle (2005) has made his ratings of gubernatorial power for the years 1980, 1988, 1994, 1998, 2001, 2004, and 2005 publicly available, and these measures could be integrated straightforwardly into comparative research on state policy for higher education.

Party Strength and Control of Governmental Institutions

Our fourth category of political-system influences on higher education policy involves partisan balance of state government. The linkage between party control of state governmental institutions and policy outcomes has been studied from a number of vantage points. Research suggests that several factors can mediate the effects of partisanship on state policy outcomes, including district-level competition, differences in the constituency bases of party support, the governing party's margin of control, and whether the party pursues policy commitments consistent with its true preferences or adjusts its positions strategically in order to attract voters (e.g., Barrilleaux et al., 2002). Nonetheless, numerous empirical studies find that party strength and control can influence the policy postures of states (Alt & Lowry, 2000; Barrilleaux et al., 2002; Berry & Berry, 1990; Holbrook & Percy, 1992; Stream, 1999; Yates & Fording, 2005). For instance, Democratic Party strength has been linked with higher levels of state taxation, higher overall spending, higher spending on certain education and welfare programs, and with abortion access and gay rights initiatives. Republicans, on the other hand, have been associated with higher levels of spending on law enforcement, higher incarceration rates, regulatory and tax policies that are viewed as more favorable to business interests, and with opposition to lotteries and abortion access.

A recent series of studies has produced intriguing evidence of connections between the partisan complexion of state government and policy outcomes in the higher education arena (McLendon et al., 2006; McLendon, Deaton, & Hearn, 2005; McLendon, Heller, & Young, 2005).[11] In all three studies, statistically significant coefficients for partisanship withstood rigorous statistical controls for state socioeconomic conditions, attributes of higher education systems, and the influence of other political-systems. Researchers in one study found Republican legislative control associated with state adoption of certain college-financing policies in the 1980s and 1990s, but found no such relationships involving accountability policies (McLendon, Heller, & Young, 2005). In a second investigation, researchers returned to the accountability arena using *event history analysis* to examine the factors that led states to adopt performance-accountability mandates from 1979 to 2002 (McLendon et al., 2006). Their analysis identified Republican legislative party strength as a primary driver of adoption, but the direction of the influence varied across the three policies studied. McLendon and colleagues also examined reforms in state governance of higher education from 1985 to 2000 (McLendon, Deaton, & Hearn, 2005). In this third study, the authors tested the "political-instability hypothesis," or the proposition that governance change is most likely to occur in states where there has been greatest turbulence in political institutions. Their event history analysis yielded strong support for the hypothesis, pointing to rates of change in Republican legislative

membership and to shifts from divided to unified party control of legislatures as predictors of the initiatives.[12]

These initial studies suggest the desirability of incorporating diverse
measures of partisan balance of government into research on higher education policy. One may wish to operationalize *partisan* influences in a
variety of ways, depending on the underlying relationships that one hypothesizes to exist. A few examples include party control of legislatures
(i.e., a binary variable designating which of the two major parties control
the institution in a given year), year-to-year changes in party control,
compositional strength (i.e., the percentage of seats across chambers of a
legislature that belongs to either of the two parties), rates of change in
compositional strength over time, and interparty competition (i.e., an indicator of the degree of competition for control of government or the
legislature). Note that indices of interparty competition, such as the Ranney index,[13] differ from more straightforward measures of partisan balance in that the former attempt to capture the degree of Democratic or
Republican control of government over time. The Ranney index also can
be recalculated to indicate the level of competition between the parties
for control of government, a subtle but important distinction (Bibby &
Holbrook, 2003).[14] All of the operationalizations noted require annual
measures of partisanship, the leading source of which traditionally has
been the *Book of the States*. Recently, Klarner (2004) made a signal contribution to the literature by organizing detailed data on the partisan balance
of state government from 1959 to 2000.

Interest Group Climates

Interest group climates represent a rich source of variation in state systems, yet higher education researchers have largely ignored rigorous study
of interest groups in policymaking. The states exhibit remarkable variety
in terms of the numbers, diversity, activities, and power of the interest
groups operating within them (Hrebenar & Thomas, 2003; Nownes &
Freeman, 1998). Traditionally, much of the work on interest groups has
sought to explain differences in lobbying styles and activities and in the
ecology of state interest-group systems—in effect treating groups as a
dependent variable. A substantial empirical literature also has arisen on
the impact of interest groups on the policy choices of states. For example,
recent work has shown that interest group strength and diversity help
shape the allocative decisions of state governments (Gray & Lowery,
1988, 1996; Jacoby & Schneider, 2001), although a host of factors (e.g.,
party strength and cohesion, governors, lobbying strategy) appear to mediate the effect (Wiggins, Hamm, & Bell, 1992). Higher education specialists have been very slow in investigating the policy impacts of state

interest group climates. A handful of case studies and cross-sectional analyses suggest the value of this line of inquiry (deGive & Olswang, 1999; Sabloff, 1997), but few rigorous and systematic across-state studies exist.

A variety of indicators of interest group strength are readily available. Despite limitations, these indicators could be readily incorporated into policy research on higher education in the states. Two such measures combine quantitative and qualitative data in a 50-state assessment of individual group influence and overall system power (Hrebenar & Thomas, 2003). The Hrebenar-Thomas ranking of the most influential interests organizes 40 interests into 3 categories, from most to least effective.[15] The analysts also developed a classification of states according to the overall impact of interest groups relative to other actors. This fivefold typology arrays states along a continuum, ranging from systems in which interest groups as a whole are the overwhelming influence on policymaking to systems in which interest groups are consistently subordinate to other actors.[16] Both rankings are based on similar sets of measures collected in 1989, 1994, 1998, and 2002, thus permitting comparisons over time.

Three other indicators, ranging from generic to higher education specific, merit discussion. First, studies have used Gray and Lowery's (1996) "relative density" variable as a measure of *general* interest group strength in a state. This variable is defined as the ratio of gross state product to the number of organizations registered to lobby within the state, with larger values indicating economically stronger groups.[17] Higher education researchers may find a second indicator even more useful. Public-agency officials often are the most effective advocates for specific programs (Gormley, 1996; Mintrom, 1997). To account for this potential influence on the policy choices of governments, some studies have used a ratio of public-sector employees to population. Although the size of some segment of a state's bureaucracy does not necessarily translate into lobbying success, it does capture the relative prevalence of one possible source of influence on governmental behavior (Gormley, 1996). An indicator like this might be used to test hypotheses on the growth of the state higher education bureaucracy, appropriations levels and trends across sectors of higher education, state policies toward the private (or for-profit) sectors, or other policy outcomes for which the size of the labor force in public higher education could conceivably shape government's choices.[18]

McLendon, Hearn, and Deaton's (2006) recent work on the emergence of new accountability mandates for higher education suggests yet a third approach to measuring interest group influence. Their analysis revealed an inverse relationship between university-dominated governance systems and the probability of states adopting rigorous accountability mandates. Building on Lowry's (2001) work on principal-agent theory, the authors surmise that certain governance arrangements for higher education (i.e., consolidated governing boards) might advance the interests of certain stakeholders (i.e., academic) more than others (i.e., elected officials) on particular issues. Thus, the model of governance a given state practices could condition the strength of the higher education lobby relative to other political actors in the state. As suggested in our earlier discussion of Lowry's (2001) research, one advantage to viewing different governance models as distinct forms of interest group representation is the availability of a consistent set of proxy measures over time (McGuinness, 1997).

Interstate Policy Diffusion

The final category composing our framework focuses on the influences states exert upon one another—often termed policy *diffusion* pressures. Several distinct diffusion models exist. The most prevalent one holds that states are likely to emulate those neighbors with which they share a contiguous border (Berry & Berry, 1990; Mintrom, 1997). A second popular approach operationalizes one's "neighbor" as other states to which one is regionally bound (e.g., the South). Recently, scholars have begun exploring other relationships, including politico-geographic connections (e.g., distances between state capitols) and economic connections that might transcend geographical boundaries, or other networks only semi-related to geographical considerations (McLendon et al., 2006).

As noted, several studies have examined relationships between geographical regions and state policy for higher education (Hearn et al., 1996; Hossler, 1997; Volkwein, 1987; Zumeta, 1996). Yet, only recently have interstate diffusion pressures overtly been tested. These recent analyses have provided mixed evidence on diffusion. For example, analyses of state adoption of college-savings, prepaid-tuition, and merit-scholarship programs have yielded conflicting results, and studies examining accountability mandates consistently have failed to find diffusion-like effects at work (Doyle, 2005; Doyle et al., 2005; McLendon, Deaton, & Hearn, 2005; McLendon et al., 2006; McLendon, Heller, & Young, 2005).

One clear advantage to studying diffusion-like pressures is that one state's policy influence on another can be rather easily measured and incorporated into a multivariate model. Diffusion traditionally has been measured as the proportion of a state's "neighbors" that had already adopted a particular policy at the time the given state adopted the policy.

This approach seeks to capture the cumulative pressures for policy adoption arising from the prior behaviors of a state's neighbors or peers, however *neighbor* or *peer* might be defined.[19] Thus, diffusion can be measured simply by counting the number of states constituting a predetermined social network that have taken a particular action by a specific point in time. Although measurement of policy diffusion might seem straightforward, the information upon which its calculation depends might not be clear-cut or easily obtained—for reasons we discuss in the following section, determining what constitutes a "policy" and when one has been adopted can sometimes prove daunting.

Summary of the Framework

To summarize, although our framework does not purport to provide a unified theory of governmental behavior, it does encompass a set of factors we propose to be critical in state policy action in higher education. Those factors—state socioeconomic climates, political culture, and ideology, legislative organization and membership, gubernatorial influence, party strength and control of governmental institutions, interest group climates, and interstate policy diffusion—each contribute in important ways to the emergence of policy in a given state. Some do so via indirect channels. For example, the socioeconomic conditions in a state can arguably drive citizens and legislators toward certain ways of thinking, and thus toward certain policy choices. Thus, discussions preceding the development of merit-aid programs in several Southern states prominently featured attention to lagging educational quality indicators in those states. Other factors in the list suggest more direct influences. For example, when the parties in power in a state change, there is likely to be movement toward signature legislative proposals, and such proposals have often focused on education, thus suggesting a direct link from change in partisan control toward action in postsecondary policy. Regardless of the mechanisms involved, whether indirect or direct, the factors enumerated have a logical and, increasingly, an empirical rationale for inclusion in models of policy development.

Challenges of Incorporating Political Indicators into Comparative-State Study of Higher Education Policy

Clearly, there are numerous advantages in incorporating political indicators into comparative-state policy research on higher education. Yet, researchers also face notable challenges in building data sets and conducting analyses along the lines we have discussed. In the remainder of the chapter, we describe five such challenges, drawing on lessons that we have learned as a result of our own recent work.

1. *Challenges of Theoretical Relevancy.* One of the most glaring challenges in building a comparative-state research literature on the determinants of public policy for higher education involves the challenge of theoretical relevancy: What is the basis theoretically for one to presume that certain political features of the states might have distinctive connections with public policies for higher education? For example, what would be the theoretical justification for presuming that differences among states along a continuum of liberal-conservative political attitudes should help explain interstate variation in higher education funding trends, regulatory climates, or financial aid regimes? In our view, such rationales exist, they appear plentiful, and they are taking a variety of creative forms in the accumulating literature (e.g., Doyle, 2005; Hicklin & Hawes, 2004; Lowry, 2001; McLendon et al., 2006). Given our field's prior inattention to systematic political analysis, it is essential that analysts continue to build the theoretical underpinnings of this line of work.

2. *Challenges in Defining and Operationalizing the Dependent Variable.* In our work, we have confronted four challenges relating to the definition of *policy* and policy adoption. Each of these questions holds important implications for comparative research. First, what is a policy? When are the actions of governments deemed as constituting public policy—when an initiative is enacted, funded, implemented, or something else? For example, Georgia's HOPE scholarship was fully operational prior to the program's formal enactment into law. When studying longitudinally the factors associated with the creation of state merit-scholarship programs, what year in one's data set should Georgia's program be coded as date of adoption? Clearly, "policy" should be determined contextually (depending on the goals of one's study), but also consistently and with some clear rationale. Second, and relatedly, whose behavior constitutes public policy—the elected "principals" (i.e., legislators and governors), or the administrative "agents" (i.e., coordinating board officials), or both? If one chooses not to distinguish between the actions of principals and agents, how can a single explanation account equally for the behaviors of both parties, when there is evidence suggesting that elected principals and bureaucratic agents hold different goals, operate from differing

bases of authority, and respond to distinctive environmental pressures (Moe, 1987)? These challenges present in turn a third one: Because many data sources fail to define *policy* in clear operational terms, the researcher might be unable to place much confidence in reported dates of "policy adoption" for use as dependent variables. Consequently, labor-intensive searches of state statutes might be necessary to cross-validate dates of important policy activity.

A fourth challenge concerns how policies across states should be meaningfully compared and scored. Much of the research both in higher education and political science presumes that a policy is a policy is a policy—but is it? States rarely adopt identical initiatives, yet studies often fail to differentiate among similar policies on the basis of their scope or content. For example, the states' merit-scholarship programs differ significantly in their eligibility requirements and along other substantive dimensions. Differences in policy design and content provide rich opportunities for empirical analysis when viewed both comparatively and over time. To what extent are the factors associated with the adoption of more robust policies similar to the factors associated with the adoption of less robust ones? What accounts for the broadening or narrowing of policy scope over time? These questions demonstrate the important conceptual implications that can stem from simple seeming definitional matters.

3. *Challenges of Sample Selection and Delimitation.* Much of our discussion in this chapter presumes the inherent desirability of 50-state research designs—the more states the better, it would seem. There are notable advantages to this approach. Yet, the questions of which states one should study comparatively and why are not necessarily clear-cut. Ideally, sample selection should serve larger theoretical purposes and methodological necessities. It is conceivable that a sample of states (rather than all 50 of them) might provide sufficient variability along the key dimensions of interest.

Indeed, even a handful of states—or one of them alone—might prove adequate under some circumstances (Nicholson-Crotty & Meier, 2002). Truly in-depth exploration of a single state can provide richer, more grounded, and better-contextualized information. Comparisons among systems within individual states can be especially fruitful. Systems within states sometimes vary in the governance, legal frameworks, and financing policies affecting them. For example, in California, Michigan, and Minnesota, states with a constitutionally autonomous flagship institution, the research-university sector is immune from some of the political oversight present in the state-university and community college systems (Hearn, McLendon, & Gilchrist, 2004). Different public higher education sectors within a given state can have significantly different policy climates, personnel, students, missions, and funding, and those differences can also provide needed bases for comparative analysis.

A different sort of challenge involves the need for delimiting one's sample when one is faced with differences across state political systems that inhibit meaningful comparisons. For example, Nebraska's unique nonpartisan, unicameral legislature poses problems for the testing of many party-related hypotheses. Thus, studies often omit Nebraska from analyses in which partisan control is a critical theoretical consideration. What, then, does one do when relatively few dependent observations (i.e., policy adoptions) exist for a given analysis and one of those occurred in Nebraska? The researcher's dilemma becomes one of trade-offs among conceptual clarity, external validity, and statistical power. Alaska and Hawaii also can prove problematic, but for different reasons. Studies in which spatial conceptions of diffusion are hypothesized to be important policy influences often omit the two states from analysis, because they do not share a land border with the other 48 states— who, after all, is Hawaii's "neighbor?" These questions point out the need for higher education researchers to carefully weigh both theoretical and methodological considerations when choosing states to study comparatively.

4. *Challenges of Data Collection and Measurement.* The avenue of research we have outlined throughout this chapter holds substantial implications for data collection. Most studies today examining policy outcomes in the American states employ some form of longitudinal analysis. Often, the reason for doing so extends beyond the statistical problems that commonly attend cross-sectional designs (e.g., few observations; little power). For one, the time sensitivity of certain political variables suggests the need for data sets capable of capturing both spatial and temporal dimensions of policy adoption. Some facets of state political systems, such as institutional powers of governors, are unlikely to change notably over the short run. Other political-system features, such as partisan control, can change markedly in the span of a single year. State economic conditions and conditions within the higher education system itself can also fluctuate from year to year. Thus, researchers

need to develop data sets that, for each state, include *annual* indicators of the factors believed to influence the focal policy activity. Such multistate, longitudinal data sets are naturally ideal, but digging deep into conditions, processes, and issues in each state over time can pose insurmountable costs. Many of the data elements that we have discussed are now available via reliable secondary sources, but the tasks of identifying, organizing, cross-validating, and cleaning data across states and over time can be quite labor intensive.

Other data-related challenges exist. For example, one often finds data on certain political indicators covering only a brief time period. Although the Klarner-produced data files at the State Politics and Policy Data Archive now stand as a definitive source of information on partisan control of state government dating back to the 1950s, many indices of conceptually relevant variables exist only for particular years. When conducting longitudinal analysis, what are the appropriate strategies for handling missing data in such instances, so as to reduce biased estimates? Does one impute the missing values? Does one create trend curves? Does one truncate the time series (and thus one's study) to accommodate gaps in the independent-variable data? These questions indicate the major challenges awaiting researchers even when many of the needed data elements are publicly available.

5. *Challenges of Analytic Capacity.* A fifth challenge to conducting an across-state study of higher education policy involves the analytic methods required. The tools most appropriate for investigating many of the relationships we have explored in this chapter are ones often not emphasized in many graduate education programs in higher education. For example, *event history analysis* (EHA) has become the standard technique for use in studying many forms of governmental behavior. Essentially a logistic regression technique applied to grouped data over time, EHA examines both whether and when a particular event occurred, permitting the analyst to make inferences concerning the influence of certain independent variables on the duration and timing of an event (e.g., when a state adopted a particular policy). For those studying state-level policy phenomena, one distinct advantage of the technique is that the coefficient estimates EHA generates can be used to calculate probabilities that a state with certain attributes will adopt a policy in a given year (Berry & Berry, 1990; Box-Steffensmeier & Jones, 1997).

Although the technique has found application in numerous studies of college student careers (see DesJardins, 2003), only a handful of studies thus far have used EHA in examining state-level policy outcomes for higher education (Doyle, 2005; Doyle et al., 2005; McLendon et al., 2006). Other analytic techniques might also be appropriate, depending on the nature of the outcome studied (e.g., Nicholson-Crotty & Meier, 2003). Yet, thorough grounding by higher education specialists in event history analysis and in other techniques similarly well suited for analyzing the behavior of state governments over time seems essential.

Conclusion

Understanding why states do what they do is both an important and daunting conceptual and analytic challenge. The data easiest to acquire often have proven inadequate to the task. Socioeconomic and structural characteristics of states, for example, fall far short of providing adequate explanations of the adoption of certain governance, accountability, and finance reforms in higher education. Veteran political observers and leaders rarely describe activity in their states without emphasizing the role of specific political institutions, actors, and processes. Trying to squeeze meaningful inferences out of models downplaying or ignoring "politics" is, for insiders, naive at best. Political factors are decidedly not easy to incorporate into modeling, but they are crucial to valid and reliable analysis of state-level policy phenomena.

Yet, it is important to think of policy development holistically. Years of trying to explain policy by emphasizing such indirect factors as structural conditions and socioeconomic contexts have shown that, in this case at least, those factors are not enough. Similarly, "street-level" political analysis seems inadequate to the task of understanding why some states move toward certain policy choices and others don't—how, for example, would such factors account for the fact that merit-scholarship programs have emerged mainly in the Southeast? What, then, is a minimal set of factors required for productive consideration of the phenomenon at hand? In the hard sciences, the standard for quality scholarship is parsimony, sometimes termed elegance and sometimes termed, more prosaically, simplicity. One aims for nothing less than the most straightforward possible explanation of a phenomenon. Clearly, a minimal set of factors for explaining policy development must include elements of the structural, the socioeconomic, the political, and the regional contexts. To focus solely on one approach is to ignore the demands of good science. Ideally, this chapter presents a first step toward an appropriately inclusive approach. For many higher education scholars, the approaches outlined in this chapter might lie in new territory, but it is territory that must be entered.

Notes

1. Consider as evidence the advent of new college-financing policies (e.g., merit-scholarship programs), accountability mandates (e.g., performance funding), governance regimes (e.g., charter colleges), and admissions policies (Top-10 percent plans).
2. Of course, there are also many differences among the states' postsecondary systems and policies, encompassing a state's total postsecondary enrollment and its distribution among two- and four-year institutions and the public and private sectors, a state's total number of institutions and its distribution among two- and four-year institutions and public and private institutions, the nature of the state's governance system, the pricing of colleges and universities, and so forth.
3. The three leading explanations for emulative influences are that states look to their neighbors 1) as a shortcut in decision making, 2) so they can gain a competitive advantage or avoid being disadvantaged relative to their peers (e.g., the "race to the bottom" in state welfare benefits), and 3) because of competitive electoral pressures from within.
4. Year-to-year changes in the economic health of a state might be measured as three-year average change in gross state product, tax revenues, or unemployment levels.
5. Elazar's three major subcultures are moralist (predominant in New England, the upper Midwest, and the far West), individualist (comprising the Mid-Atlantic and lower Midwest regions), and traditionalist (primarily the South and Southwest).
6. Researchers sometimes have placed statistical controls on "region," reasoning informally along the same lines as Elazar, if without explicit link to the particular ideas underlying Elazar's work.
7. Similar arguments appeared previously in work by Zumeta (1996).
8. Lowry classified states as practicing one of several basic models of statewide governance of higher education, based on the McGuinness (1997) typology.
9. One advantage of this approach is the availability of the McGuinness governance typology, which could be used to assign states values representing the degree of control by governors.
10. But see Dometrius's (1979) critique of the Schlessinger index.
11. See also Nicholson-Crotty and Meier (2003) and Volkwein (1987).
12. *Divided government* refers to the condition that exists when the legislative and executive branches of a state are held by different political parties, or when one legislative chamber is held by one party and the other chamber and the executive are held by the other party. Much research has arisen on the

policy effects of divided government (Alt & Lowry, 2000; Huber, Shipan, & Pfahler, 2001).

13. This index, developed in the 1970s by Austin Ranney, uses three different components to measure partisan control of government: proportion of electoral success, duration of success, and frequency of divided control. A score of 0 indicates complete Republican control and a score of 1 indicates complete Democratic control (Ranney, 1976). As noted, the index has subsequently been recalculated to capture a variety of other political phenomena in the states.

14. Recently, Holbrook and Van Dunk (1993) developed a measure of electoral competition, which includes an index based on district-level, state legislative election outcomes. Their district-level measure has been shown to be a better predictor of policy in states than the Ranney index.

15. The most recent assessment, in 2003, placed colleges and universities as the 20th most effective individual interest overall. This aggregate score is somewhat misleading; colleges and universities ranked among the "least effective" interest in more than one-half of the states.

16. The existence of the two measures raises the possibility of interactions: To what extent do powerful individual interests in weak overall interest-group systems shape policy differently than do singularly powerful groups operating in strong overall group systems?

17. Gray and Lowery have argued that this ratio is the most appropriate measure of group strength because it captures the "average economic base behind interest organizations in a state" (1996, p. 89).

18. Data on higher education's share of the state workforce is available in the *Book of the States*.

19. Some older diffusion approaches pursued so-called leader-laggard models, whereby dates of adoption are factor analyzed to determine which conditions lead states to adopt policies earlier in time than other states.

References

Alt, J. E., & Lowry, R. C. (2000). A dynamic model of state budget outcomes under divided partisan government. *Journal of Politics, 62*(4), 1035–1069.

Barrilleaux, C., & Bernick, E. (2003). "Deservingness," discretion, and the state politics of welfare spending, 1990–1996. *State Politics and Policy Quarterly, 3*, 1–18.

Barrilleaux, C., Holbrook, T., & Langer, L. (2002). Electoral competition, legislative balance, and state welfare policy. *American Journal of Political Science, 46*(2), 415–427.

Berry, F. S., & Berry, W. D. (1990). State lottery adoptions as policy innovations: An event history analysis. *American Political Science Review, 84*(2), 395–416.

Berry, W. D., Ringquist, E. J., Fording, R. C., & Hanson, R. L. (1998). Measuring citizen and government ideology in the American states, 1960–93. *American Journal of Political Science, 42*(1), 327–348.

Berry, W. D., Ringquist, E. J., Fording, R. C., & Hanson, R. L. (2004). *Measuring citizen and government ideology in the United States. ICPSR Study No.: 1208.* [Data file]. Available from Inter-University Consortium for Political and Social Research Web site, http://webapp.icpsr.umich.edu/cocoon/ICPSR-PRA/01208.xml

Beyle, T. (2003). The governors. In Gray, V. & Hanson, R. L. (Eds.), *Politics in the American states* (8th ed.) (pp. 194–231). Washington, DC: CQ Press.

Beyle, T. (2005). *Gubernatorial power: The institutional power ratings for the 50 governors of the United States.* [Data file]. www.unc.edu/~beyle/gubnewpwr.html

Bibby, J. F., & Holbrook, T. M. (2003). Parties and elections. In Gray, V., Hanson, R. L., & Jacob, H. (Eds.), *Politics in the American states* (pp. 66–110) Washington, DC: CQ Press.

Box-Steffensmeier, J., & Jones, B. (1997). Time is of the essence: Event history models in political science. *American Journal of Political Science, 41*(4), 1414–1461.

Brace, P., & Jewett, A. (1995). The state of state politics research. *Political Research Quarterly, 48,* 643–681.

Carey, J. M., Niemi, R. G., & Powell, L. W. (2001). *Term limits in the state legislatures.* Ann Arbor: University of Michigan Press.

Center for American Women and Politics. (2005). *Number of women in office: State summaries,* (2005) [Data file]. Available from Center for American Women and Politics, Eagleton Institute of Politics, Rutgers University Web site, www.cawp.rutgers.edu/ Facts/StLegHistory/stleghist.pdf

Council of State Governments. (2004). *The book of the states.* Lexington, KY: Council of State Governments.

Dawson, R. E., & Robinson, J. A. (1963). Inter-party competition, economic variables, and welfare policies in the American states. *Journal of Politics, 25*(2), 265–289.

deGive, M. L., & Olswang, S. (1999). Coalition building to create a branch campus system. *The Review of Higher Education, 22*(3), 287–313.

DesJardins, S. L. (2003). Event history methods. In Smart, J. (Ed.), *Higher education: Handbook of theory and research* (Vol. XVIII, pp. 421–472). London: Kluwer.

Dilger, R. J., Krause, G. A., & Moffett, R. (1995). State legislative professionalism and gubernatorial effectiveness, 1978–1991. *Legislative Studies Quarterly, 20*(4), 553–571.

Dometrius, N. (1979). Measuring gubernatorial power. *Journal of Politics, 41,* 589–610.

Dometrius, N. (1987). Changing gubernatorial power: The measure vs. reality. *Western Political Quarterly, 40,* 320–328.

Doyle, W. R. (2005). The adoption of merit-based student grant programs: An event history analysis. Unpublished manuscript available at www.vanderbilt.edu/lpo/doyle/research.htm

Doyle, W. R., McLendon, M. K., & Hearn, J. C. (2005, November). *The adoption of prepaid tuition and savings plans in the American states: An event history analysis.* Paper presented at the annual meeting of the Association for the Study of Higher Education.

Dye, T. R. (1966). *Politics, economics, and the public.* Chicago: Rand McNally.

Dye, T. R. (1990). *American federalism: Competition among governments.* Lexington, MA: Lexington Books.

Elazar, D. J. (1966). *American federalism: A view from the states.* New York: Thomas Crowell.

Erikson, R., Wright, G., & McIver, J. (1993). *Statehouse democracy: Public opinion and policy in the American states.* New York: Cambridge University Press.

Eulau, H., & Quinley, H. (1970). *State officials and higher education.* New York: McGraw-Hill.

Fitzpatrick, J. L., & Hero, R. (1988). Political culture and political characteristics of the American states. *Western Political Quarterly 41,* 145–153.

Gormley, R. (1996). Accountability battles in state administration. In Van Horn, C. (Ed.), *The state of the states* (3rd ed.) (pp. 161–178). Washington, DC: CQ Press.

Gray, V. (2003). The socioeconomic and political context of states. In Gray, V., & Hanson, R. L. (Eds.), *Politics in the American states* (8th ed.) (pp. 1–31). Washington, DC: CQ Press.

Gray, V., & Lowery, D. (1988). Interest group politics and economic growth in the U.S. states. *American Political Science Review, 82*(1), 109–131.

Gray, V., & Lowery, D. (1996). *The population ecology of interest representation.* Ann Arbor: University of Michigan Press.

Hays, S. P. (1996). Influences on re-invention during the diffusion of innovations. *Political Research Quarterly, 49*(3), 631–650.

Hearn, J., & Griswold, C. (1994). State-level centralization and policy innovation in U.S. postsecondary education. *Educational Evaluation and Policy Analysis, 16*(2), 161–190.

Hearn, J. C., Griswold, C. P., & Marine, G. (1996). Region, resources, and reason: A contextual analysis of state tuition and student aid policies. *Research in Higher Education, 37*(1), 241–278.

Hearn, J. C., McLendon, M. K., & Gilchrist, L. Z. (2004). *Governing in the sunshine: Open meetings, open-records, and effective governance in public higher education.* Monograph prepared for the Association of Governing Boards of Universities and Colleges and the Center for Higher Education Policy Analysis of the University of Southern California.

Heller, D. E. (1997). Student price response in higher education: An update to Leslie and Brinkman. *The Journal of Higher Education, 68*(6), 625–659.

Hicklin, A., & Hawes, D. (2004, April). *Hopwood and Proposition 209: Judicial and legislative intervention in American higher education.* Paper presented at the annual meeting of the Midwest Political Science Association, Chicago, IL.

Holbrook, T., & Percy, S. (1992). Exploring variations in state laws providing protections for persons with disabilities. *Western Political Quarterly, 45,* 191–220.

Holbrook, T. M., & Van Dunk, E. (1993). Electoral competition and the American states. *American Political Science Review, 87,* 955–962.

Hossler, D., Lund, L., Ramin, J., Westfall, S., & Irish, S. (1997). State funding for higher education: The Sysyphean task. *Journal of Higher Education, 68*(2), 160–190.

Hrebenar, R., & Thomas, C. (2003). Interest groups in the states. In Gray, V., & Hanson, R. L. (Eds.), *Politics in the American states* (8th ed.) (pp. 111–143). Washington, DC: CQ Press.

Jacoby, W. G., & Schneider, S. K. (2001). Variability in state policy priorities: An empirical analysis. *The Journal of Politics, 63*(2), 544–568.

Jewell, M. E., & Whicker, M. L. (1994). *Legislative leadership in the American states.* Ann Arbor: University of Michigan Press.

Joint Center for Political and Economic Studies (2005). *Joint center databank.* www.jointcenter.org/DB/index.htm

Katz, E., Levin, M., & Hamilton, H. (1963). Traditions of research in the diffusion of innovations. *American Sociological Review, 28,* 237–252.

Klarner, C. (2004). *Measurement of partisan balance of state government.* [Data file]. State Politics and Policy Data Resource. Available from www.unl.edu/SPPQ/ journal_datasets/klarner.html

Knott, J., & Payne, A. (2004). The impact of state governance structures on management and performance of public organizations: A study of higher education institutions. *Journal of Policy Analysis and Management, 23*(1), 13–30.

Lowry, R. C. (2001). Governmental structure, trustee selection, and public university prices and spending. *American Journal of Political Science 45*(4), 845–861.

McGuinness, A. C. (1997). *State postsecondary education structures handbook.* Denver, CO: Education Commission of the States.

McLendon, M. K. (2003). State governance reform of higher education: Patterns, trends, and theories of the public policy process. In Smart, J. (Ed.), *Higher education: Handbook of theory and research* (Vol. 18, pp. 57–143). London: Kluwer.

McLendon, M. K., Deaton, R., & Hearn, J. C. (2005, November). *The enactment of state-level governance reforms for higher education: A test of the political-instability hypothesis.* Paper presented at the Association for the Study of Higher Education, Philadelphia, PA.

McLendon, M. K., Hearn, J. C., & Deaton, R. (2006). Called to account: Analyzing the origins and spread of state performance-accountability policies for higher education. *Educational Evaluation and Policy Analysis, 28*(1), 1–24.

McLendon, M. K., Heller, D. E., & Young, S. (2005). State postsecondary education policy innovation: Politics, competition, and the interstate migration of policy ideas. *The Journal of Higher Education, 76*(4), 363–400.

Mintrom, M. (1997). Policy entrepreneurs and the diffusion of innovation. *American Journal of Political Science, 41,* 738–770.

Mintrom, M., & Vergari, S. (1998). Policy networks and innovation diffusion: The case of state education reforms. *Journal of Politics, 60,* 126–148.

Moe, T. (1987). An assessment of the positive theory of "Congressional dominance." *Legislative Studies Quarterly, 12,* 475–520.

Mohr, L. (1969). Determinants of innovation in organizations. *American Political Science Review, 63*(1), 111–126.

Moncrief, G., Thompson, J., & Cassie, W. (1996). Revisiting the state of U.S. state legislative research. *Legislative Studies Quarterly, 21,* 301–335.

Mooney, C. Z., & Lee, M. H. (1999). Morality policy reinvention: State death penalties. *Annals of the American Academy of Political and Social Sciences, 566,* 80–92.

Nicholson-Crotty, S., & Meier, K. P. (2002). Size doesn't matter: In defense of single case studies. *State Politics and Policy Quarterly, 2*(4), 411–422.

Nicholson-Crotty, J., & Meier, K. J. (2003). Politics, structure, and public policy: The case of higher education. *Educational Policy, 17*(1), 80–97.

Nownes, A. J., & Freeman, P. (1998). Interest group activity in the states. *Journal of Politics, 60,* 86–112.

Oppenheimer, B. J. (1985). Outputs of legislatures. In Patterson, S. (Ed.), *Handbook of legislative research* (pp. 551–597). Cambridge, MA: Harvard University Press.

Ranney, A. (1976). Parties in state politics. In Jacob, H., & Vines, K. (Eds.), *Politics in the American states* (pp. 34–65). Boston: Little Brown.

Rizzo, M. J., & Ehrenberg, R. G. (2004). Resident and nonresident tuition and enrollment at flagship state universities. In Hoxby, C. (Ed.), *College choices: The economics of where to go, when to go, and how to pay for it* (pp. 303–354). Chicago: University of Chicago Press.

Rogers, E. (1962). *Diffusion of innovations.* New York: The Free Press.

Sabloff, P. L. (1997). Another reason why state legislatures will continue to restrict public university autonomy. *Review of Higher Education, 20*(2), 141–162.

Schlesinger, J. A. (1965). The politics of the executive. In Jacob, H., and Vines, K. (Eds.), *Politics in the American States* (1st edition) (pp. 207–231). Boston: Little, Brown, and Company.

Sharkansky, I. (1969). The utility of Elazar's political culture. *Polity, 2,* 66–83.

Soss, J., Schram, S., Vartanian, T. P., & O'Brien, E. (2001). Setting the terms of relief: Explaining state policy choices in the devolution revolution. *American Journal of Political Science, 45*(2), 378–395.

Squire, P. (1992). Legislative professionalization and membership diversity in state legislatures. *Legislative Studies Quarterly, 17*(1), 69–79.

Squire, P. (2000). Uncontested seats in state legislative elections. *Legislative Studies Quarterly, 25*(1), 131–146.

Squire, P., & Hamm, K. (2005). *101 chambers: Congress, state legislatures, and the future of legislative studies.* Columbus: Ohio State University Press.

Stream, C. (1999). Health reform in the states. *Political Research Quarterly 52*(3), 499–525.

Thomas, S. (1991). The impact of women on state legislative policies. *Journal of Politics, 53*(4), 958–976.

Volkwein, J. F. (1987). State regulation and campus autonomy. In Smart, J. (Ed.), *Higher education: Handbook of theory and research* (Vol. III, pp. 120–154). New York: Agathon Press.

Walker, J. L. (1969). The diffusion of innovations among the American states. *American Political Science Review, 63*(3), 880–899.

Wiggins, C., Hamm, K. E., & Bell, C. G. (1992). Interest group and party influence agents in the legislative process: A comparative state analysis. *Journal of Politics, 54,* 82–100.

Yates, J., & Fording, R. (2005). Politics and state punitiveness in black and white. *Journal of Politics, 67*(4), 1099–1121.

Zumeta, W. (1996). Meeting the demand for higher education without breaking the bank. *The Journal of Higher Education, 67*(4), 367–425.

CHAPTER 2

Can Access to Community Colleges for Low-Income Adults Be Improved?

Testing a Model of the Policy Change Process Across Six Diverse States

Kathleen M. Shaw and Thomas Bailey

Is it possible to develop a single model of policy change that applies across multiple and diverse states? Under what circumstances might this be possible? In 2002, the Ford Foundation embarked on the Bridges to Opportunity Initiative (Bridges), which seeks to promote state policies that enhance the capacity of community college systems to improve the educational and economic opportunities for low-income adults on a large scale. Working with Colorado, Kentucky, Louisiana, New Mexico, Ohio, and Washington, the foundation is in its third year of a five-year effort to achieve these goals.

The Bridges to Opportunity Initiative uses a model of the process of policy change that focuses on the engagement of a wide variety of constituencies with an economic or social interest in increasing access to education for low-income adults (Colburn & Driver, 2002). This conceptual model hypothesizes that the involvement of a broad range of stakeholders, from local advocacy organizations and businesses to state-level departments of workforce development and labor, will provide the political pressure needed to elicit relevant policy at the state level and to change institutional practice at the local level.

A team of researchers based at the Community College Research Center at Teachers College, Columbia University, is examining the implementation of the Bridges to Opportunity Initiative in each of the six states and is analyzing as well the salience of the change model that was developed by the Ford Foundation and serves as the guiding set of ideas undergirding the initiative. The work of the evaluation team, which has been ongoing since 2002, is the basis of this chapter. Although the purpose of the chapter is not to provide a formal evaluation of the Bridges project, it does use this project as a lens through which to examine the promises and limitations of using theory as a guide to the analysis of policy implementation across multiple states.

The Bridges to Opportunity Model of Policy Change

The Bridges to Opportunity Initiative organizers have developed a strategy to create the state-level policy changes and the institutional-level practices needed to increase access to community colleges for low-income adults. The organizers believe that this outcome will be brought about through a policy change model (see figure 2.1) that emphasizes the change process by identifying a series of steps and players necessary to achieve the desired change. As can be seen in figure 2.1, the first step in the policy change process involves the engagement of key stakeholders in the goals of the Bridges Initiative at both the state and the local levels. The term *stakeholder* is defined quite broadly in this model and encompasses a range of individuals, local and grassroots organizations, community college faculty and administrators, local businesses, and relevant state-level policymakers and legislators. The engagement of this broad group of interested parties is expected to lead to political pressure at multiple levels,

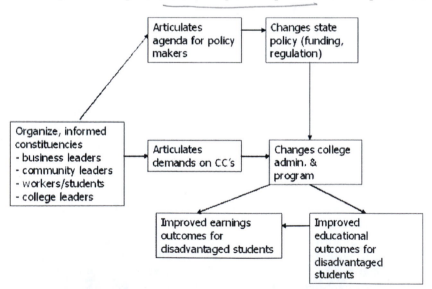

Figure 2.1 Bridges to Opportunity Theory of Change Model.
Source: Cyrus Driver and John Colburn, The Ford Foundation

which in turn will result in changes in state policy that create both an entry and a pathway through college for the target population.

At a more operational level, in order to be successful, these changes must occur at both relevant state agencies and in community colleges. Although the model could support a variety of operational and programmatic initiatives, it does emphasize the integration of services across state agencies, as well as across curriculum areas in community colleges. The underlying assumption is that community college students would be better served if state agencies overseeing the two- and four-year higher education systems, the workforce development systems, and services such as Adult Basic Education (ABE) and English as a Second Language (ESL) worked more closely together. Similarly, at the college level, the Bridges project encourages better coordination between mainstream academic and occupational credit education and promotes better coordination among these and programs such as ABE and ESL and other noncredit programs designed especially to serve low-income students. A sophisticated use of data, especially to track student progress using unit records, is a key part of the strategy, because it can be used to support mobilization of stakeholders, identify opportunities to improve policy and practice, and assess the eventual effectiveness of strategies. Thus the Bridges strategy to strengthen community college service to low-income students can be summarized as follows: Stakeholders can be successfully engaged through the use of good data and information, this engagement will lead to policy change that will support service integration at both the state and the institutional levels, and the effectiveness of this integration will be demonstrated by sophisticated data analysis based on statewide student tracking systems. This evidence will in turn support and fuel further system integration changes and will ultimately improve access and retention for low-income adults.

The six states engaged in the Bridges project receive a modest amount of funding per year—between $100,000 and $200,000. In addition, they receive technical assistance in a range of areas, including data systems, public relations and media, and policy development. A team of evaluators also conducts site visits in each state and provides annual feedback to the states and to the Ford Foundation. In addition, each year there are at least two annual meetings for all project participants, each of which focuses on a specific subject (e.g., finance).

The Challenges of Theorizing the Policy Change Process

The realm of public policy is a notoriously difficult one to study. The sheer complexity of the policy change process does not allow for static or one-dimensional studies; instead our understanding of it is best advanced by those studies that track and attempt to explain the myriad factors involved in policy change in a dynamic and iterative fashion. As John (2003) notes in his comprehensive review of public policy theory:

> Public policy . . . tends to include in its baseline *all* political activity and institutions. . . . In addition, decision making varies vastly from sector to sector . . . which complicates the task at hand. The problem is compounded by the absence of a clear chain of causation from public opinion to parties and bureaucracies and back again. (p. 483)

As a result, developing a model of policy change that takes into consideration both the complexity of the process *and* the variability of context is extremely challenging. Developing a model of change that has any explanatory power when used *across* states is doubly difficult (Sabatier, 1999). Importing theories from specific disciplines, such as political science, is also problematic, since they are often not well suited for the dynamic nature of policy change (John, 2003).

The Study of Policy Change Processes in an Age of Devolution

A 2004 special issue of the journal *Public Administration,* comprising articles from an international symposium entitled "Implementing Public Policy: Learning from Theory and Practice," makes a number of points relevant to the question of whether it is possible to apply a general model of policy change across multiple states attempting to change higher education policy. Policy change and implementation theorists generally fall into two broad categories—those that adopt a "top-down" view that emphasizes how centralized policy is diffused to local levels and the "bottom-uppers," who are more attuned to stakeholder groups and other grass-roots organizations that exist outside of formal government structures but who nevertheless can exert influence on the policy change and implementation process (Barrett, 2004). A recent comprehensive review of both schools of thought by O'Toole (2004) identifies shortcomings in both approaches to policy theory when taken alone; he states that each has "a tendency to caricature the influence of either central or contextual actors, respectively" (p. 322). This critique suggests that using both approaches in tandem could provide the most robust analysis. Exworthy and Powell (2004) go farther than this, arguing that top-down models of policy theory that privilege the "vertical" or "silo" relationships linking a central state agency with multiple local counterparts is inappropriate. Rather, changing models of governance require a far more complex and multilayered policy process than has been needed in years past. Drawing on Weber's notion of an "ideal type" of bureaucracy, Exworthy and Powell argue that in order for top-down policy theory to be relevant, there must exist "a unitary organization with clear lines of authority, such as the army" (p. 264). Absent such a structure, we must draw our attention to models that allow for the study of "horizontal collaboration" (Hill & Hupe, 2002), which examine how multiple organizations, both within state governance structures (e.g., state agencies) and outside of them (e.g., interest groups), interact to develop and implement policy.

The Bridges to Opportunity model of change clearly incorporates both a bottom-up and a top-down approach to examining the implementation of its policy change model. With its dual emphasis on state- and institutional-level integration, along with an explicit recognition of the interaction between and among both local and state-level stakeholders, this change model allows for an unusually nuanced analysis of the change process.

What Is the Appropriate Role of Theory in Cross-State Policy Change Studies?

Yet the degree to which theory informs or improves policy practice is open to debate. O'Toole (2004) points out that the core assumption of theory-building is that "valid theory can inform and improve practice by offering knowledge that can be tapped by people in the world of action" (p. 311). However, the exact nature of the relationship between the two remains unclear when it comes to the policy arena.

There are a number of reasons for this ambiguity. First, at a very general level, policy change agents—that is, those individuals who are responsible for both translating and enacting policy—are not a monolithic group. Nor do they respond or interpret policy in a uniform manner, a fact that gained broad notice with the publication of Lipsky's *Street-Level Bureaucracy* in 1980. In short, "expecting some theory, any theory, to translate simply into a clear and uniform body of knowledge suitable for all such customers is to expect far too much" (O'Toole, 2004, p. 312).

Second, much policy—and particularly higher education policy—is developed and enacted in multiple contexts. This has become particularly true in the wake of a national policy trend called devolution that has emerged in the last decade or so, in which states are expected to interpret and implement federal policy (Weaver, 2000). As a result, there is wide variation in how policy is actually developed and in how it is played out on the ground. Examples of this phenomenon include the variations and difficulties in state interpretations of No Child Left Behind, as well as in state efforts to enact financial aid, accountability, and other higher education policies (McLendon, Heller, & Young, 2005). Moreover, there are very few empirical studies of state higher education policy innovation. Those that do exist (Hearn & Griswold, 1994; McLendon et al., 2005) shed important light on the factors that predict or contribute to state higher education policy change. But because they focus on identifying determinants of policy innovation, rather than on an understanding of how determinants work together to form a policy innovation *process*, they cannot fully illuminate the complexity of policy change. In short, the question of whether a generalizable model of higher education policy change is possible is one that has not yet been answered in a definitive manner.

We use the interim results of our ongoing evaluation of the Bridges initiative to begin to address this question. The purpose of the evaluation has been twofold: first, to determine whether states are making progress toward the end goal of increasing educational and economic outcomes for low-income adults; and second, to determine whether the model of change is robust. Over the past three years, we have gathered a wide array of information in each state from a variety of sources, including: annual two- to three-day site visits in each state by researchers from the Community College Research Center (CCRC), review of documents related to Bridges activities, participation in Bridges conferences in 2004–2006, and discussions with Ford program officers and an array of technical assistance providers. Detailed assessments of each state are developed annually, and these individual assessments, along with cross-state analyses, serve as the basis of the analyses presented here.

Analysis of the Bridges Policy Change Model

Although the Bridges to Opportunity model of policy change is somewhat complex because of the multiple relationships that are hypothesized to exist among and between elements of the model, here we focus on four major components of the model: stakeholder engagement, policy development, mission integration at both the state and institutional levels, and outcomes tracking. In doing so, we present an analysis of the factors that affect whether states are making progress on implementing each part of the model; and we assess as well whether the states are responding to the Bridges initiative in a similar manner.

Stakeholder Engagement

Stakeholder engagement is a fundamental component of the Bridges model. In theory, a wide array of individuals and organizations with interest in the goal of increasing access to community colleges for low-income adults is the major engine that will drive change. As stakeholders become convinced of the need for more access to community colleges, they will in turn pressure legislators and other policymakers to enact the state and local policy changes needed to achieve this goal.

Yet the activities in our states suggest that it is much easier to engage some stakeholders than others. In most of the six states, the groups directly engaged are those inside the community and technical college world, related agencies (e.g., human service, workforce or economic development agencies), and politicians. For example, the state of Louisiana has recently merged its community and technical colleges, but its attempts to move forward with their Bridges agenda have been hampered by influential state legislators who have difficulty envisioning an effective and vibrant community college system. As a result, Louisiana has used most of its Bridges funding to gather these legislators and other relevant decision makers to take them to model community college systems in other states. These informational study trips have uniformly been reported to be of great import by Louisiana's Bridges team members; legislators who had previously resisted the merger of the community and technical college systems now have a much clearer understanding of its potential, and some have become advocates for further supporting policy. However, there has been little attention paid to engaging a broader, more diverse range of stakeholders.

The State Board of Community and Technical Colleges (SBCTC) in Washington has also focused much of its attention on developing stakeholder support among politicians and community college leadership in that state as well. Over the past year, the presidents and public information officers from the 34 Washington community and technical colleges collaborated on a strategic communication plan designed to increase awareness of and support for the colleges locally and also build support for the colleges among state policymakers; yet the target of this campaign is not grassroots organizations advocating for the poor, nor is it the poor themselves.

There are exceptions to this rule among the Bridges states. Ohio has assembled a 50-member stakeholder group that includes representation from the community colleges, adult career centers, state agencies, community organizations, and employer associations. These stakeholders have brought a focus on low-income adult workers to the discussion of policies related to adult and postsecondary education, workforce, and economic development. One of the governor's staff persons told us that this process has built "a sense of mutual trust and shared mission" among groups that formerly did not talk with one another. Yet in most states, the Bridges projects have not emphasized engaging outsiders such as community organizations, advocates, and others that directly represent the interests of low-income students.

Nor have stakeholders tended to be the primary drivers of change in most states, despite the fact that the model of change posits them as such. For example, the state of Kentucky worked first at the state policy level and then at the institutional level to develop examples of how community colleges could better serve low-income adults. This state decided to use Bridges funding to develop a grant program for individual community colleges to develop "career pathway" curricula that create bridges between the technical and academic sides of the community college enterprise. The apparent initial success of some of these pilot efforts are being used to build support for the Bridges initiative more broadly, and the state is garnering the support of an increasing array of stakeholders who had not previously been involved in the Bridges Initiative. Thus, although there is a relationship between stakeholders and action at the state and institutional levels, the "causal path" is not as linear or as clear as the Bridges model of change would suggest. Indeed, in the case of Kentucky, we see a state whose strategy has been to enact change in the system first and then to use these successes to develop stakeholder engagement—not the other way around.

Interim Policy Development

In some states, policy development supporting the Bridges Initiative is occurring at a pace more rapid than would be expected given the proposed model of change. For example, the state of Ohio was able to quickly achieve a legislative victory with the passage of a bill that provided funding to strengthen the opportunities for students completing industry-certified, noncredit coursework in adult career centers to transfer to any state institution of higher education.

In contrast, owing to forces well outside the purview of the Bridges project, policy development is difficult in Louisiana. Senior Louisiana Community and Technical College System (LCTCS) staff have spent much of their time fending off attempts to weaken the system by state legislators interested in retaining their control over local technical colleges. Although there was hope that adult literacy would be moved to the postsecondary sector, it is now clear that it will remain with K–12, which hampers the initiative's efforts to comprehensively address the education and training needs of low-income adults (of which approximately 20 percent are illiterate). It has been difficult for the Louisiana team to move forward on policy issues, because they have been engaged in a rearguard action designed to preserve the unification of the community and technical college system. The series of events that occurred in the wake of Hurricane Katrina have only made this task more difficult.

In another example, the New Mexico Association of Community Colleges provided the Bridges leadership in that state, but flux in the association has slowed down the progress of the project. Some concrete proposals did emerge, such as a proposal to broaden access to the state's lottery-based scholarship and smooth the transition from adult basic education to credit programs. Yet conflict within the association has jeopardized the chances of achieving the goals of the Bridges Initiative.

Mission Integration

Mission integration is an integral part of the Bridges model, because it is seen as a necessary precondition for achieving the long-term goals of the initiative (see figure 2.1). It can be thought of as an interim policy outcome, in that increased access to college for low-income adults is unlikely to occur without mission integration at both the state and the institutional levels—a fact that we will discuss in more detail. At the state level, mission integration is broadly conceptualized to include activities designed to build ties between community and technical college agencies and other state-level agencies concerned with education, social services, workforce, and economic development. At the local level, the focus is on creating stronger articulation among the remedial, workforce, and transfer mission areas within colleges and strengthening connections with the labor market, further education, and feeder education systems outside colleges.

State-Level Mission Integration. There is no concrete, well-defined model of service integration at the state level to guide states participating in the Bridges Initiative. In fact, states participating in the Bridges Initiative vary dramatically on these efforts because of such factors as whether the state has a centralized higher education or community college system, whether some level of state integration was already in existence, whether there is a history of agencies working well together, and whether the political climate is volatile. For example, both Kentucky and Washington have strong systems of community colleges, as well as a history of coordinating well with other relevant agencies. Because of this strong foundation, these states have not had to work as hard as others to establish a baseline level of coordination and integration.

In contrast, Ohio's recent success in mandating greater cooperation between the Ohio Department of Education, which oversees the adult career centers (as well as the K–12 education system), and the Ohio Board of Regents promises to increase articulation between credit and noncredit courses. But this success took considerable effort, owing to the fact that the state does not have a centralized system of community colleges. Although Louisiana does have a newly created community and technical college system, a volatile political climate has required the Bridges team to devote nearly all of their efforts toward preventing state-level *dis*integration of the system. Thus, our focus on the policy development process suggests that previous studies detailing the strong and positive effect of higher education systems on policy innovation (McLendon et al., 2005; Hearn & Griswold, 1994) might not have captured the complex and changeable interaction among these systems and other relevant factors.

Institution-Level Mission Integration. In contrast to integration at the state level, the Bridges Initiative is using a very well-defined model for achieving mission integration at the institutional level. The Career Pathways model (Jenkins, 2004) is designed to create bridges between the academic and career/technical sides of community colleges, allowing courses that traditionally do not bear academic credit to count toward a degree or certificate. Too, the Career Pathways model requires community colleges to work closely with the local labor market to identify areas of employment that will provide both immediate employment and a long-term career trajectory.

There is clear indication of progress on institutional-level integration in some states. Ohio and Kentucky are providing support for community and technical colleges to create career pathways. Multiple community colleges are participating in this activity in both states; yet the emphasis is more on strengthening relationships among community and technical colleges and outside entities and the labor market than on internal reforms. In both cases, a key challenge is how to involve faculty in developmental and academic transfer programs in programs that also have a strong workforce emphasis.

Most of the other states participating in Bridges have not been active in developing institutional- or local-level mission integration. However, the inclusion of this aspect in the Bridges Initiative is being used to encourage policy development in two different ways. First, the Ford Foundation regularly holds meetings that bring together Bridges teams from all six states, and these meetings are used to disseminate knowledge and lessons from states that are moving more quickly toward implementing the Career Pathways model and other elements of institutional-level mission integration. This strategy is in keeping with recent work documenting policy migration across states (McLendon et al., 2005). In addition, as pilot Career Pathways projects are implemented in individual community colleges in Kentucky and Ohio, the energy and enthusiasm for these efforts are being used to drive state policy. Thus, although not planned for, a feedback loop of sorts between local- and state-level integration activities appears to be occurring, and aspects of model dissemination across states is happening as well.

Tracking Outcomes

According to the Bridges model of change, data collection and dissemination is a critical lever with which to engage stakeholders and, ultimately, argue for major policy changes at both the state and institutional levels. It is particularly important that states are able to disaggregate data so as to understand the challenges faced by at-risk groups and to track students' progress within and across systems of higher education—and into the employment sector.

In general, although all participating states are interested in using data in this way, the degree to which they can do so is uneven. Information emerging from our fieldwork, as well as additional work conducted by the National Center for Higher Education Management Systems, the Community College Research Center, and Jobs for the Future, indicates that most states already have much more relevant data than they are using. Yet political and bureaucratic barriers, reinforced by legal restrictions, prevent the integration of data sets necessary to allow tracking of students from high school through higher education and into the labor market. For example, enrollment funding systems do not create incentives for states or colleges to track student outcomes. In general, most states collect data to meet the requirements of particular funding streams. In some states, particularly New Mexico, concerns about the Family Educational Rights and Privacy Act (FERPA), which is designed to protect the privacy of U.S. citizens, have thwarted data sharing and made it difficult to analyze student progress, particularly from one level of education to the next.

Traditional bureaucratic divisions and, sometimes, mistrust have also slowed data integration efforts. These factors partially explain why the regents and the Department of Education do not share data in Ohio; and in Washington state, competition between the two- and four-year systems has slowed efforts to share data and conduct joint analysis. Finally, most states do not have the human and fiscal capacity at both the state and institutional levels to analyze data for purposes of informing improvements in policy and practice rather than simply for compliance and accountability.

For example, our analysis of states' data capacity indicates that Washington has by far the best community college data in terms of its scope and its availability when compared with the other states in our study. However, the state's K–12 data are not of high quality, hampering efforts to analyze high school to community college movements. Links between the two- and four-year systems are possible, but still cumbersome, and work is being done to improve this link. The state of Colorado has begun to implement a new data system that will be able to track students at both the individual community college level and at the system level; but, as in Washington, students in Colorado cannot be followed across sectors. However, the data system will enable the state to disaggregate the data. In fact, legislation requires that data are reported on a range of populations that are designated "underserved"—low-income, nonwhite, and male.

In contrast, the absence of a state higher education system in New Mexico until quite recently creates significant difficulties in attempts to develop integrated data systems. Yet the state created a Higher Education Department in 2005, which replaced the former New Mexico Commission on Higher Education and in doing so granted much more centralized control and coordination over the state's public higher education institutions. This development could provide new opportunities for New Mexico to move forward in constructing a comprehensive data system. In short, although strengthening the state data systems has clearly become a priority for the Bridges Initiative, state progress on this goal varies because of capacity and structural and resource issues.

Conclusions, Lessons, and Questions

Although there is not the space in this chapter to review in detail how well each state is enacting the Bridges model of change, we have attempted to provide enough information to give a general sense of the political, structural, and resource factors that can restrict or alter a state's efforts in this regard. It is important to note that, as of this writing, the Bridges to Opportunity Initiative is still developing in many ways. Given the time-consuming legislative process and the difficulties of implementation, any statewide initiative can be expected to take several years to be fully operational, therefore, it is too early to fully assess the degree to which the model of change has been carried out or whether the initiative is capable of being fully implemented in any of the six states. Still, our initial analyses allow us to identify a range of issues that are relevant to the central question guiding this chapter—namely, is it possible to develop a general model of policy change that is applicable across a range of diverse state contexts?

Clearly, if the question before us is whether the Bridges model of policy change is being strictly implemented as described in figure 2.1, the answer is no. Although the project is still unfolding, it is not too early to assess whether the change *process* in each state is adhering to the model. And it is clear that the project is not rolling out as hypothesized in the theoretical model of change.

To support this analysis, we point to the relationships among the various elements of the model in figure 2.1. As we described earlier, the model posits that stakeholder engagement, fueled and supported by persuasive data, will exert pressure on state-level policy, leading to mission integration at the state level. As states coordinate their efforts around mission integration, they exert pressure on community colleges, as do stakeholders. From there, the model posits that mission integration at the institutional level occurs, as community colleges work with local agencies to create career pathways attractive to both low-income adults and the local economy.

Yet our analysis of the six states clearly indicates that the relationships among the model elements vary considerably. For example, in some states there is only a narrow group of stakeholders engaged in the initiative, whereas in other states a broader and more diverse group of stakeholders has become involved. Moreover, the degree of stakeholder involvement varies by state, with some playing a relatively small role in the initiative and others being intimately involved in the planning and implementation of the initiative. Some states must collect a significant amount of persuasive data in order to engage stakeholders, whereas in other states they have been present from the start. There is little doubt that at least some level of stakeholder engagement is a necessary ingredient for lasting policy change in the Bridges Initiative. However, the specific role of stakeholder engagement, and in particular its relationship with the other elements of the change model, varies by state.

To take another example, state-level policy is hypothesized to drive change at the local or institutional level. Yet in at least two states, institutional-level mission integration pilot projects are commanding the attention and energy of individuals and agencies at the state level, and the promise of these efforts is being used to initiate or further the state-level policy change needed for the initiative to be sustained over the long term.

In short, it does not appear that the model of change that drives the Bridges Initiative is a generalizable model of state policy change. As Schofield and Sausman (2004) assert, context most assuredly does matter when thinking about the relationship between theory and state-level policy change, and a variety of contextual factors makes it highly unlikely that the elements of policy change will interact in the same way across diverse states.

Among the most important contextual factors affecting the implementation of the Bridges model of change are the following:

1. **Political and administrative instability.** Bridges activities in at least four states have been influenced by political changes in the state or changes in the management and makeup of the Bridges team. The initiative in Colorado has undergone a profound change, one that, if funding for higher education in Colorado can be stabilized, has some promising elements. And management change in the Bridges New Mexico team might have brought the initiative there more in line with broader Bridges objectives. It is too strong to say that these projects are starting over, because current activities are taking place in the context of the relationships and discussions that took place during earlier phases; nevertheless, these events have created significant discontinuities in the work of those two states.

   New governors with new priorities in Louisiana and Kentucky have changed the environment for Bridges in those states at the state level. These changes have tended to reinforce the emphasis in Kentucky on local or institutional change as a way to keep the initiative moving. In Louisiana, state-level change in governance seems to have been associated with a reopening of the issue of technical college integration—a major barrier to progress on Bridges.

   Bridges is an initiative designed to influence state policy, and yet the politics and the players in state capitals often change. Hence, as much as possible, the Bridges teams should make plans that are not dependent on a particular set of political circumstances or officeholders.

2. **The capacity of state data systems.** Although it would be naive to assume that data, in and of itself, has the power to compel serious policy change, there is little doubt that if used effectively, data can be a powerfully persuasive tool in the policy change process. However, weaknesses in the data systems of each state hamper the effectiveness of this tool. Developing a robust and comprehensive statewide data system that provides necessary linkages among K–12, postsecondary, and labor/employment systems requires enormous resources, political will, and technical skill. States that

have relatively effective postsecondary data systems and a sophisticated knowledge of how to use them, such as Washington, are more successful in persuading policymakers to adjust policy than are states without such capacity.

3. **Higher education governance structures.** State-level community college governance structures can greatly affect whether, and how, policy change is achieved. Of the six states involved in the Bridges Initiative, Washington and Kentucky have well-established, stable community and technical college systems. These systems have enabled these states to engage in a wide array of policy activity prior to the Bridges Initiative, and as a result, both states had a significant base upon which to build.

In contrast, although Louisiana and Colorado also have community college systems, both have been under siege during the first few years of the Bridges Initiative, which has rendered them less effective in advancing or overseeing Bridges policy changes. The other two states—Ohio and New Mexico—have operated without a centralized community college system (although New Mexico did establish a Department of Higher Education in 2005). This does not necessarily mean that the states will be less effective in implementing the Bridges model; in fact, the state of Ohio is arguably the most successful of the six states thus far. However, what variation in state governance systems *does* mean is that the policy change process will vary and that states need to plan accordingly.

Policy Change Theory as a Heuristic Device

Theory is often thought of as inflexible and prescriptive; elements of a theoretical model must work in the way specified in order for the model to be seen as legitimate. According to these strict standards, the Bridges to Opportunity model of policy implementation and change cannot be considered a robust one. As O'Toole (2004) points out, policy theories are most often not predictive in the narrow sense of the word, and the Bridges model is no exception. As noted previously, there are simply too many contextual variations to make such a relationship possible.

However, if we think about theory in a more heuristic sense that provides a broad outline of relevant aspects of the policy change process rather than a detailed and inflexible recipe that must be followed in order to achieve success, the Bridges to Opportunity model of change has real utility. Our analyses certainly suggest that the major ingredients for policy change are present in this model; in fact, as noted earlier, the model is unusually comprehensive in its inclusion of both bottom-up and top-down factors that operate in the policy implementation process. Moreover, if we were to remove the connective and unidirectional arrows that specify the relationships between and among the variables, we would find that we could use these variables to construct a unique change model for each of the six states. Each model would include the specified elements in the Bridges theory of change; but the exact definition of each, the sequence of events, as well as the relationships between and among them, would vary according to context. In short, there is a role for theory in conducting comparative-state policy change. Yet we must reach beyond conventional conceptions of the relationship between theory and practice.

How could we construct a study of the application of theory to state policy change in higher education that provides a more realistic recognition of the variation across states that does occur? First, theory that guides state policy implementation in the realm of higher education must provide enough room for variation among and between elements of the change model. Documenting these variations is the only way for such studies to provide any utility to the field of policy research. Approaching the study of policy change as an inductive process—that is, collecting data and adjusting policy implementation theory accordingly—is optimal. In this way, a general policy change model can be adjusted to reflect the reality of varying state contexts.

Second, such studies should pay attention to both top-down and bottom-up levers of policy change. Incorporation of such elements into policy implementation theory is clearly necessary in the case of cross-state higher education policy study, as our analysis of the implementation of the Bridges Initiative suggests.

Third, the study process itself must allow for the dynamic nature of the policy change process. Multiple site visits over time, multiple points of quantitative data collection, triangulation of data sources—all are necessary elements of the study of policy change processes in general, and are particularly important when trying to make sense of higher education policy diffusion from state to local levels.

As John (2003) points out, "when considering about how to theorize about public policy, there are two things to bear in mind. One is the nature of theory in the social sciences; the other is the character of public policy" (p. 482). Whereas theory is designed to be predictive and generalizable, public policy is maddeningly variable, subject to a broad range of influences. Yet if those interested in using theory in the comparative study of state-level higher education policy are willing to redefine theory as a more flexible set of guideposts that identify relevant areas of study in the policy change process, we have much to learn.

References

Barrett, S. M. (2004). Implementation studies: Time for a Revival? Personal re-
flections on 20 years of implementation studies. *Public Administration, 82*(2),
249–262.

Colburn, J., & Driver, C. (2002). *The bridges theory of change.* New York: Ford
Foundation.

Exworthy, M., & Powell, M. (2004). Big windows and little windows: Implementation in the "congested state." *Public Administration, 82*(2), 263–281.

Hearn, J. C., & Griswold, C. P. (1994). State-level centralization and policy innovation in U.S. postsecondary education. *Educational Evaluation and Policy
Analysis, 16*(2), 161–190.

Hill, M., & Hupe, P. (2002). *Implementing public policy.* London: Sage.

Jenkins, D. (2004). *A bridge to community college career programs for adults
with poor basic skills.* Accessed in June 2006 at www.uic.edu/cuppa/gci/
about/bios/documents/A%20Bridge%20to%20Community%20College%
20Career%20Programs%20for%20Adults%20with%20Poor%20Basic%20
Skills.pd

John, P. (2003). Is there life after policy streams, advocacy coalitions and punctua-
tions?: Using evolutionary theory to explain policy change. *The Policy Studies Journal, 31*(4), 481–498.

Lipsky, H. (1980). *Street-level bureaucracy: The dilemmas of the individual in
public service.* New York: Russell Sage Foundation.

McLendon, M., Heller, D., & Young, S. P. (2005, July/August). State postsecondary policy implementation: Politics, competition and the interstate migration
of policy ideas. *Journal of Higher Education, 76*(4), 363–400.

O'Toole, L. T. (2004). The theory-practice issue in policy implementation research. *Public Administration, 82*(2), 309–329.

Sabatier, P. (1999). The need for better theories. In Sabatier, P. (Ed.), *Theories of
the Policy Process* (pp. 1–17). Boulder, CO: Westview.

Schofield, J. & Sausman, C. (2004). Symposium on implementing public policy:
Learning from theory and practice. *Public Administration, 82*(2), 235–248.

Weaver, K. (2000). *Ending welfare as we know it.* Washington, DC: Brookings
Institution Press.

CHAPTER 3

The Role of Higher Education in State Budgets

Jennifer A. Delaney and William R. Doyle

At the beginning of the millennium higher education faced huge budget cuts, and institutions scrambled to make up for lost state funding. Tuitions skyrocketed, and budget cuts seemed inevitable. Today in spring 2006, state budgets are recovering and higher education is slowly regaining its appropriations base. Change seems to be the only constant in state funding of higher education. Is this rollercoaster ride typical of state funding for higher education? What role does higher education play in state budgets? Why is higher education funding so volatile?

One explanation of higher education funding patterns originated by Harold Hovey, a former budget officer and expert on state finance, argues that higher education serves as a "balance wheel" for state finances. When states' revenues are low, higher education is an attractive option for heavy cuts, because it has the ability to collect fees for its services (an ability lacking in most other major state spending categories). When states' revenues are high, higher education is a politically attractive area on which to spend money (Hovey, 1999). "In bad times, state lawmakers use public higher education to balance their budgets, knowing that the institutions can raise tuition rates. Then, in good times, lawmakers funnel money back to the colleges to make up for the down years. It has worked that way for decades" (Selingo, 2003).

Literature Review

The literature on the political business cycle has established both the theoretical and empirical support for the idea that policymakers respond in a systematic way to both economic and political pressures (Nelson, 2000; Nordhaus, 1975; Rogoff, 1990). Over the long term, these responses can be recognized as part of an ongoing pattern of change in state policy.

In this chapter, we suggest that higher education as a matter of government consumption occupies a second-order spot in the political business cycle. Whereas in the classic political business cycle models, elected officials attempt to manipulate policies in order to change the direction of the economy, in the areas of state policy considered in this chapter, we assume that politicians are reacting to a preexisting economic condition—either an economic boom or a recession.

During a boom cycle, all government consumption will be favored, but competition for spending and ideological restraints imposed by coalitions will limit the ability of legislators to spend as much as they would prefer on their favored budget categories. Higher education is unique in that it has a very small, predefined constituency relative to other spending areas. For example, there is no analogy in higher education to a strong union presence from such groups as prison guards or teachers. This works to higher education's advantage during boom cycles, as politicians can agree on spending for higher education as "the least objectionable option." Standard Euclidean and Downsian voting models would both suggest that the policy area that is least disfavored should do the best during this period of the political cycle (Clinton, Jackman, & Rivers, 2004; Downs, 1957).

During a downturn, cuts will be necessary. In this instance, the same logic that benefited higher education during booms will hurt higher education during recessions. The area that is least disfavored for increases will also be the area that is most favored for decreases, since there is no strong constituency to act as a brake on spending cuts. The easy availability of an alternative revenue source, namely, tuition, only makes the situation worse for higher education.

Previous empirical literature has considered the relationship between higher education appropriations and outside forces that lead to revenue constraints in state budgets. For example, Okudade (2004) shows that the lagged level of state indebtedness is a strong predictor of the share of appropriations devoted to higher education. Considering a similar outside force, Humphreys explains how higher education appropriations are positively related to changes in the business cycle (2000). Betts and McFarland (1995) found that an increase in unemployment rates leads to an increase in enrollment demand at community colleges.

As did earlier theorists of the political business cycle (Nelson, 2000; Nordhaus, 1975; Rogoff, 1990), we suggest that policymakers are responding rationally to cyclical changes in the economic situation of the state. We differ from earlier theorists in focusing on a particular spending area (higher education) and suggesting a structural relationship between policymaker's decisions on spending and the underlying economic cycle.

Finally our approach considers the interaction between higher education and other budget categories. Using competing interest theory, Okudade (2004) shows that Medicaid competes with higher education, but corrections spending augments higher education appropriations. Likewise, Kane, Orszag, and Gunter (2003) describe how Medicaid spending crowds out spending on higher education. Significantly, K–12 education also competes with higher education for state appropriations (Toutkoushian & Hollis, 1998).

Situated in the theoretical context of the political business cycle, the outside forces that constrain state budgets, and trade-offs between budget categories, this chapter considers the structural dimensions of the role of higher education in state budgets. We suggest that higher education, in receiving both larger cuts and bigger increases than other categories, depending on the budgetary status of the state, serves as a "balance wheel" for state budgets.

Testing the Role of Higher Education in State Budgets

In this chapter we use an empirical analysis to consider whether changes in higher education funding are consistent with a balance wheel framework. Specifically we seek to answer the research question: *Do state appropriation patterns provide evidence that higher education acts as a balance wheel for state budgets?*

Higher education is funded from a number of different sources. For purposes of this chapter, we focus on state appropriations granted to public higher education by state governments over the 1990s. Over this time period, state appropriations were the primary source of funding for most public institutions, comprising approximately 50 percent of their revenue (United States Department of Education, 2001).

We focus on individual states as the unit of analysis for this study. Every year (or biennium) state policymakers must determine a way to allocate available revenues to each budget category. In addition, every state (except Vermont) must pass a budget that has no deficit. Hovey (1999) suggests that, in order to balance each state budget, policymakers rely on expenditures in the category of higher education as a balance wheel.

Hovey's Hypothesis

In formal terms, Hovey's hypothesis sets out a relationship between changes in expenditures for higher education and changes in expenditures for all other state budget categories. He suggests that the magnitude of the change in higher education funding has a greater absolute value than changes in all other categories, in both good times and bad. In other words, as changes in spending for all other categories decline, changes in spending for higher education are expected to decline even farther. As the change in spending for all other categories increases, the change in spending for higher education is expected to increase even faster.

Two forces cause higher education to be used as a balance wheel for state budgets. First, higher education has the ability to raise outside revenues from students and their families in the form of tuition and fees, as well as from private sources. Since this option is not available to most other state agencies, higher education becomes a target for budget cuts from the state. Second, because of its political attractiveness and the benefits it provides to constituents, higher education will also be the beneficiary of large budget increases in good times.[1]

What Would Higher Education as a Balance Wheel Look Like?

To begin to formalize the meaning of a balance wheel, it is first important to define what we mean by good and bad times. Intuitively, good times would mean lots of money for everyone and bad times would mean universal budget cuts. To help formalize these definitions, we created figure 3.1, a graph that places higher education appropriations on the y-axis and appropriations to all other budget categories on the x-axis. The upper right-hand quadrant in figure 3.1 represents "good times"—when appropriations to higher education increase *and* appropriations to other budget categories increase. In contrast, "bad times" are years in which appropriations to higher education decrease, as do appropriations to all other budget categories. Bad times are represented by the lower left-hand quadrant of figure 3.1.[2]

Hovey's hypothesis states that in good times appropriations to higher education would increase faster than other budget categories. Because of the increasing rate, the curve in the upper right-hand quadrant would look like the right arm of a positive quadratic function. More formally, the curve in the upper right-hand quadrant (good times) would be concave up such that when state budgets are increasing the second derivative would be positive (when $x > 0$, $f''(x) > 0$). In addition, Hovey's hypothesis states that in bad times appropriations to higher education would decrease faster than other budget categories. Because of the decreasing rate, the curve in the lower left-hand quadrant would look like the left arm of

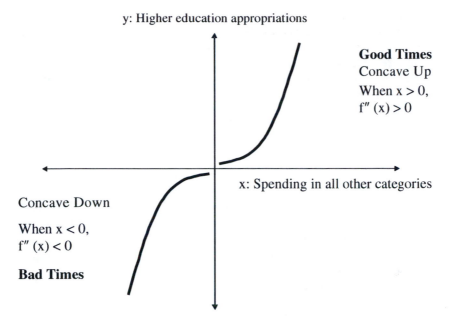

y: Higher education appropriations

Good Times
Concave Up
When x > 0,
f″ (x) > 0

x: Spending in all other categories

Concave Down

When x < 0,
f″ (x) < 0

Bad Times

Figure 3.1   The Hovey Balance Wheel Hypothesis.

a negative quadratic function. More formally, the curve during bad times (in the lower left-hand quadrant) would be concave down such that when x < 0, f″(x) <0. Combining the higher education appropriations curve in good and bad times, figure 3.1 depicts an S-shaped curve that represents Hovey's hypothesis.

This S-shaped curve is most parsimoniously described as a cubic function (which would have the general mathematical form: $y = a + bx + cx^2 + dx^3$ (where b and d are positive). Although other higher-order functions (for example quartic or quintic functions) might also have an S-shape, we think the cubic function most closely fits Hovey's hypothesis (and his intent), because it is the simplest form that fits his description. Similarly, a linear function, which has a second derivative of zero, cannot fully describe the balance wheel model. Hovey's hypothesis suggests that the shape of the curve needs to be nonlinear, since the relationship of funding to changes in expenditures for other categories relates not just to increases or decreases, but rather to the rate of change in these increases or decreases. Since higher-order functions are not parsimonious and linear functions cannot describe variations in year-to-year changes in higher education funding, we think that the cubic function best describes Hovey's hypothesis.

In our empirical test of Hovey's hypothesis, we are looking for three things: first, that the cubic model offers the best fit of the data; second, that the second derivatives of the function conform to the balance wheel model as defined previously; and third, that the trend in state budgeting forms an S-shaped curve when inspected graphically. If we find that our data for higher education appropriations conform to these three characteristics, then we will have found evidence in support of Hovey's hypothesis.

Finally, Hovey's hypothesis should *only* apply to higher education. If other state budget categories follow the same pattern of an S-shaped, cubic function, then this is a general principle of budgeting and not descriptive of a balance wheel for higher education. We therefore estimate the model outlined previously for other state spending categories in order to understand the relationship between state spending for these categories and the rest of the state.

In this chapter we consider state spending for three other spending categories that are often thought to be in competition with higher education for state funding: K–12 education, corrections, and health care (Kane et al., 2003; Okudade, 2004; Toutkoushian & Hollis, 1998). Each of these areas of state expenditures comprises a significant amount of state spending. Combined, these categories accounted for nearly 60 percent (59.6%) of state general fund expenditures in fiscal year 2004 (National Association of State Budget Officers, 2005). In addition, each is thought to have a "traditional," or linear, relationship with state spending; in other words, increasing at a steady rate in good times and decreasing at a steady rate in bad times. Hence, the final indication that Hovey's hypothesis is correct is that the cubic form of the polynomial will *not* be the preferred model for any of the other categories of state spending.

Data

Our study makes use of data collected for all 50 states for the years 1991–1999.[3] Descriptive statistics for the variables used in the analysis can be found in table 3.1. Our variables are defined as follows.

- State appropriations for higher education per capita: This data is collected in a yearly survey conducted by the Center for the Study of Education Policy at Illinois State University (Center for Higher Education and Educational Finance, 2002).
- State expenditures (total, K–12 education, health, and corrections) per capita: State expenditure data is collected by the Census Bureau, as part of the Census of State and Local Governments. We make use of Census Bureau data because of common definitions of state

Table 3.1   Descriptive Statistics for Variables in Analysis
(Standard deviations in parentheses)

	Mean 1991	Mean 1999
Appropriations for higher education per capita	389.12 (800.75)	407.13 (788.72)
State spending for K–12 education per capita	22.30 (125.31)	27.93 (143.12)
State spending for health per capita	84.40 (44.95)	111.23 (63.1)
State spending for corrections per capita	82.55 (33.99)	117.40 (39.26)
State expenditures per capita	3,443.47 (767.06)	4,061.96 (720.64)
State revenues per capita	3,658.40 (753.21)	4,803.75 (1352.61)
Percent of the population aged 18–24	10.30 (.069)	9.52 (1.08)
Percent of the labor force unemployed	6.44 (1.54)	4.12 (1.01)

Note: All variables are adjusted for inflation using the CPI-U. Reported values are in 1999 dollars.

budget categories used across states and across years (United States Department of Commerce, Bureau of the Census, 2002).

- State revenues per capita: We use state own-source revenues from the Census of State and Local Governments (United States Department of Commerce, Bureau of the Census, 2002).
- Percent of the population aged 18–24: These data are from the Census Bureau (United States Department of Commerce, Bureau of the Census, 2003).
- Unemployment: We use definitions and measures from the Bureau of Labor Statistics (United States Department of Labor, Bureau of Labor Statistics, 2003).

All monetary data in the data set are adjusted for inflation using the Consumer Price Index for all urban consumers (CPI-U) and are reported in 1999 dollars (United States Department of Labor, Bureau of Labor Statistics, 2004).

Model

Because we are concerned in this chapter with year-to-year changes in appropriations for higher education, all variables will be expressed as first differences:

$$\Delta y_{it} = y_{it} - y_{it-1}$$

Beyond being directly relevant to our theory by allowing us to capture the change in appropriations for higher education, the use of first differencing simplifies our estimation, because it implements a fixed-effects model for the panel data that we use. The model to be estimated is:

$$\Delta y_{it} = \alpha + \beta_1 \Delta x_{it} + \beta_2 \Delta x_{it}^2 + \beta_3 \Delta x_{it}^3 + \Delta z_{it} + \Delta w_{it} + \Delta v_{it} + \epsilon$$

where:
  y = State appropriations to higher education
  x = Expenditures in all other categories
  z = Revenues for the state
  w = The number of 18–24-year-olds in the state
  v = Percent unemployment for a state

In addition to changes in state expenditures, these models also include three supplementary variables to control for other possible causes of change in state spending for higher education. First, the change in state revenues is included in each model (represented by the z variable). This controls for any possible changes in state finance that might affect higher education beyond the change in expenditures for that year for all other categories. Second, the change in the proportion of the population aged 18–24 is included in each model (represented by the w variable). This controls for any changes in the demand for higher education that might affect the levels of state spending for higher education per capita. Last, changes in unemployment levels are also included (represented by the v variable). This variable is entered into the model to control for any possible shifts in the economic situation of the state that might or might not change state spending for higher education.

Because this is a first-differences model, Ordinary Least Squares (OLS) can be used to return estimates (Wooldridge, 2003). By first differencing all of the data, we define a model that only looks at relationships between changes in one variable and changes in another variable. For instance, the simplest version of our model looks at the amount of change experienced by higher education appropriations as a function of the amount of change in the overall level of expenditures for the state as a whole. The coefficients in this model do not have the normal interpretation of a unit of change in state expenditures, resulting in a certain change in higher education appropriations. Instead, the interpretation of our results must be done in the context of rate of change—a unit change in change in expenditures will result in a certain change in the change in appropriations for higher education.

The first differencing structure also means that we will drop one year of data, as nine years of data only imply eight differences to estimate in the panel data set. In addition, we eliminated the state of Alaska from the data, as it was a consistent outlier on nearly every variable in the analysis. This leaves us with 392 observations (49 states $\times$ 8 differenced years) for the analysis.

For each of the budget categories, we use F-tests to see if the model fit is significantly improved by the addition of higher-order terms. Next, with the coefficients we found in our estimation, we find the second derivative to test conformity to the balance wheel model. Finally, we graph the function to visually inspect for an S-shaped curve.

Results

Table 3.2 presents results for the regression of state appropriations for higher education on the independent variables mentioned above. First, the F-tests reveal that the model 3 (the cubic model) offers the best model fit. The F statistics for the joint null hypothesis (that all coefficients are 0) for all three models suggests that we can reject the null hypothesis at conventional levels. In addition, an F-test restricting the variables to include only the quadratic form suggests that the inclusion of a cubic term significantly increases model fit. As the table shows, the coefficient for the cubic term for change in state expenditures is positive and the coefficient for the squared term is negative. Both are statistically significant ($p < .01$). The reader will note the small R^2 values returned for almost all models estimated. We were not surprised by this finding, as the relationships we are attempting to model involve year-to-year changes in state budget categories. Given the amount of complexity involved in predicting how much a given budget category in a given state will change based on a set of predictors, we expected that we could explain only a small amount of the overall variance in the dependent variables.

Second, we find evidence of conformity to the balance wheel model through our second derivative test. The results are presented in table 3.3. Surrounding an inflection point, where the curve changes from being convex to concave, of $211,667, higher education conforms to the model of a

Table 3.2   Results of OLS: Dependent Variable = per Capita Appropriations for Higher Education (Standard errors in parentheses)

	Model 1	Model 2	Model 3
Intercept	−1.63	−1.31	4.02
	(4.02)	(4.06)	(4.23)
Change in revenues (in 1,000s)	−1.00	−0.91	1.15
	(8.06)	(8.07)	(7.95)
Change in young population	2.33	1.76	1.47
	(14.85)	(14.89)	(14.63)
Change in unemployment	11.82**	11.82**	12.32**
	(4.29)	(4.29)	(4.22)
Change in expenditures (in 1,000s)	99.23**	107.12**	75.75**
	(20.14)	(23.88)	(24.87)
Change in expenditures^2 (in 10,000s)		−0.34	−2.54**
		(0.56)	(0.80)
Change in expenditures^3 (in 100,000s)			0.04**
			(0.01)
σ	57.42	57.47	56.48
R^2	0.08	0.08	0.12
F	8.64	6.98	8.45
DF	4 and 387	5 and 386	6 and 385
N	392	392	392

** = $p < .01$

balance wheel. Since $211,667 is a small value in state budgeting discussions, we consider this inflection point to be close to zero. In good times, when state expenditures are rising, the second derivative is positive indicating that the curve is concave up. In bad times, when states are cutting their budgets, the second derivative is negative indicating that the curve is concave down. Hence, other than at small values close to zero, we find support for the Hovey hypothesis through the second derivative test as well.

The third factor that we look for in support of the Hovey hypothesis is to see if the curve has an S-shape. A simulation using the results from table 3.2 is shown in figure 3.2. The simulation involves using the estimated coefficients to provide predictions for values of change in higher education spending as a result of changes in state spending for all other

Table 3.3 Results of Models 1–6: First and Second Derivatives and Inflection Points

	Higher Education	K–12 Education	Health Care	Corrections
Function	$f(x) = 0 + 12.32v + 0w + 0z + 75.75x - .254x^2 + .0004x^3$	$f(x) = 0 + 0v + 0w + 0z + 0x + .051x^2 - .0068x^3$	$f(x) = 0 + 0v + 0w - 4.46z + 22.5x + 0x^2 + 0x^3$	$f(x) = 3.11 - 0v + 0w + 0w - 0z + 12.2x + 0.21x^2 + 0x^3$
First Derivative	$f'(x) = 75.75 - .508x + .0012x^2$	$f'(x) = .102x - .0204x^2$	$f'(x) = 22.5$	$f'(x) = 12.2 + .042x$
Second Derivative	$f''(x) = -.508 + .0024$	$f''(x) = .102 - .0408x$	$f''(x) = 0$	$f''(x) = .042$
Inflection Point	$f''(x) = 0$ $211.667 = x$ If $x < 211.667$ then, $f'(x) < 0$ If $x > 211.667$ then, $f'(x) > 0$	$f''(x) = 0$ $2.5 = x$ If $x < 2.5$ then $f''(x) > 0$ If $x > 2.5$ then $f''(x) < 0$	N/A	N/A

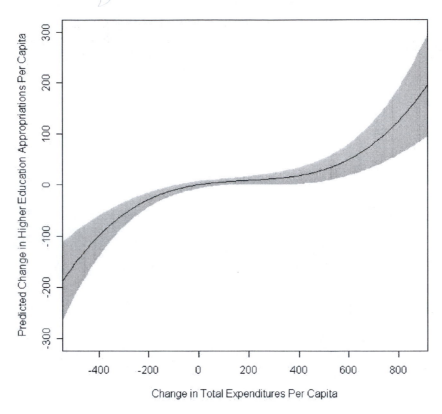

Figure 3.2   Simulated Change in Spending on Higher Education per Capita as Related to Change in Total State Spending per Capita.
Source: Table 3.2, Model 3. All other variables held at mean value.

categories. The solid line in figure 3.2 presents predicted values for changes in higher education for hypothetical changes in state spending for all other categories. The gray region indicates the 95 percent confidence interval for the prediction. Figure 3.2 shows that higher education appropriations form an S-shaped curve when graphed, which also lends support to the Hovey hypothesis.

These results provide general support for Hovey's hypothesis for higher education appropriations. Our hypothesis stated that the cubic form of the polynomial would provide the best fit to the data. We find that the cubic form does indeed fit the available data well.[4] In addition, we found that the second derivative conforms to the balance wheel model, and our simulation shows that the curve has the expected S-shape.

We also find that higher education's cuts in bad times are more severe than higher education's increases in good times. This result may have implications for the ongoing discussions of higher education funding, since it means that not all of the cuts that happen during recessions are being made up during good times.

Our study thus far has provided substantial support for the first part of the balance wheel hypothesis: that the pattern of higher education appropriations fits the balance wheel model. Next we consider if this model fits for spending categories in three additional areas: K–12 education, health care, and corrections.

Testing the Balance Wheel Model in Other Budget Categories: K–12 Education

Table 3.4 reports estimates for our three models analogous to those reported for higher education, with the dependent variable now being state spending for K–12 education. The key independent variable remains spending on all other budget categories. The F-tests indicate that the cubic form (model 3) fits the data significantly better than either the quadratic (model 2) or linear forms (model 1). As with the results from the models for higher education, the F statistic for excluding the cubic term is highly significant, indicating a statistically significant increase in model fit. This suggests that the cubic polynomial is the best fit for K–12 education, which would indicate that K–12 education serves as a balance wheel. However, there are key differences between the results for K–12 and the balance wheel model. Looking at the second derivative of the cubic form, our second test of the Hovey hypothesis, we find that K–12 education does not conform to the model of a balance wheel. This result is shown in detail in table 3.3.

Figure 3.3 graphically depicts a simulation using the results from table 3.4. As can be seen in the figure, the shape of the function for K–12, although a curve, does not have the predicted S-shape of a balance wheel. As figure 3.3 shows, it appears that negative changes (cuts) in all other categories are actually associated with slight increases in spending for K–12 education. In fact, a $500 cut in spending for all other categories is associated with a $30 increase for K–12 education. On the other hand, a $500 increase in state spending in all other budget categories results in essentially no change in per capita expenditures for K–12 education. Even though the cubic model fits the data better than other models, the second derivative does not conform to the expected form, and the curve for K–12 spending does not take the expected S-shape. Hence, spending for K–12 education does not appear to serve as a balance wheel in state budgets.

Table 3.4   Results of OLS: Dependent Variable = State Spending for K–12 Education (Standard errors in parentheses)

	Model 1	Model 2	Model 3
Intercept	1.26	1.06	0.13
	(0.79)	(0.80)	(0.83)
Change in revenues (in 1,000s)	−0.92	−0.95	−1.42
	(1.44)	(1.43)	(1.41)
Change in young population	1.34	1.54	1.68
	(2.75)	(2.74)	(2.69)
Change in unemployment	0.82	0.83	0.74
	(0.76)	(0.75)	(0.74)
Change in expenditures (in 1,000s)	0.28	−3.14	3.13
	(3.65)	(4.15)	(4.45)
Change in expenditures^2 (in 10,000s)		0.16	0.51**
		(0.09)	(0.14)
Change in expenditures^3 (in 100,000s)			−0.68**
			(0.20)
σ	9.31	9.28	9.10
R^2	0.01	0.02	0.06
F	0.43	0.93	2.85
DF	4 and 282	5 and 281	6 and 280
N	287	287	287

** $= p < .01$

Testing the Balance Wheel Model in Other Budget Categories: Health Care

Table 3.5 shows results for the regression of changes in state spending for health care on the set of independent variables mentioned earlier. The results of the F-tests indicate that changes in health spending are best predicted by a linear model (model 1), with change in spending on health care bearing a proportional relationship to changes in spending for other categories. F-tests for restricting the model from either the cubic or the quadratic form suggest no significant increase in model fit when these terms are included. The second derivative is zero, indicating that health care conforms to a linear function and does not fit the balance wheel model, as can be seen in table 3.3.

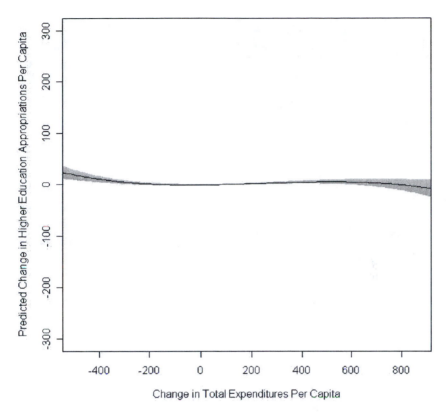

Figure 3.3 Simulated Change in Spending on K–12 Education by Change in Total State Spending.
Source: Table 3.4, Model 3. All other values held at mean or mode.

Figure 3.4 plots the hypothetical relationship of health care expenditures to all other expenditures. The figure shows a linear relationship. Hence, all of three of our tests indicate that health care does not serve as a balance wheel in state budgets.

Testing the Balance Wheel Model in Other Budget Categories: Corrections

Table 3.6 reports the same model as applied to spending on corrections. The *F*-tests indicate that the quadratic form (model 2) is the best fit in this case since an analysis of variance indicates that there is a significant decrease in model fit when the model is restricted to the simple linear model. Linear restrictions on the cubic model demonstrate no significant

Table 3.5   Results of OLS: Dependent Variable = State Spending for Health Care (Standard errors in parentheses)

	Model 1	Model 2	Model 3
Intercept	1.95	1.89	1.62
	(1.05)	(1.06)	(1.12)
Change in revenues (in 1,000s)	−4.34*	−4.35*	−4.46*
	(2.10)	(2.10)	(2.11)
Change in young population	−1.54	−1.43	−1.42
	(3.86)	(3.88)	(3.88)
Change in unemployment	−0.48	−0.48	−.50
	(1.12)	(1.12)	(1.12)
Change in expenditures (in 1,000s)	22.42**	20.90**	22.5**
	(5.24)	(6.22)	(6.59)
Change in expenditures^2 (in 10,000s)		0.07	.18
		(0.15)	(.21)
Change in expenditures^3 (in 100,000s)			−.02
			(.03)
σ	14.95	14.96	15.01
R^2	0.05	0.05	0.05
F	4.99	4.02	3.78
DF	4 and 387	5 and 386	6 and 385
N	392	392	392

* = $p < .05$
** = $p < .01$

increase in model fit when including the cubic term. As shown in table 3.3, the second derivative is a positive constant, which indicates a quadratic form and does not conform to the balance wheel model.

Figure 3.5 shows the hypothetical relationship of corrections to all other expenditures. The figure shows that spending on corrections does not conform to the S-shaped curve that would be found in a balance wheel relationship. Our three tests indicate that the corrections spending category does not serve as a balance wheel for state budgets.

Summary

Our study has documented two important findings. First, we have provided support for the beginning part of the Hovey hypothesis. Higher

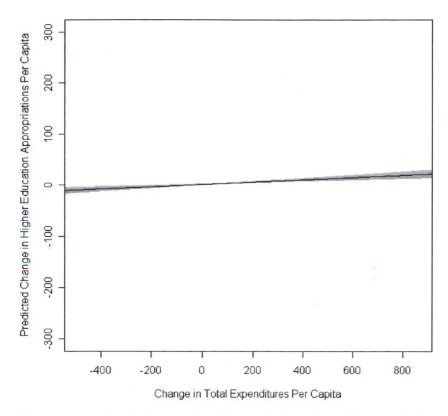

Figure 3.4 Simulated Change in Spending on Health Care by Change in Total State Spending.
Source: Table 3.5, Model 1. All other values held at mean.

education does indeed fit the model of a balance wheel. The cubic model offers a good fit, the second derivative test reveals the expected form, and, upon visual inspection, the curve has the expected *S* shape. In other words, higher education receives greater increases than other budget categories in good times and is cut more than other budget categories in bad times.

In addition, we found support for the second part of the Hovey hypothesis. Other state spending categories do not fit into the balance wheel model. We have shown that in the case of K–12, corrections, and health care, the balance wheel relationship does not appear to hold. Rather, other state budget categories have a linear relationship with state spending or, as in the case of K–12 education, have a relationship that is more complex than the balance wheel model.

Table 3.6   Results of OLS: Dependent Variable = State Spending for Corrections (Standard errors in parentheses)

	Model 1	Model 2	Model 3
Intercept	3.21**	2.96**	3.11**
	(0.71)	(0.71)	(0.75)
Change in revenues (in 1,000s)	−2.27	−2.34	−2.28
	(1.42)	(1.41)	(1.41)
Change in young population	4.04	4.5	4.49
	(2.61)	(2.59)	(2.60)
Change in unemployment	−1.25	−1.25	−1.24
	(0.75)	(0.75)	(0.75)
Change in expenditures (in 1,000s)	19.42**	13.08**	12.2**
	(3.54)	(4.16)	(4.41)
Change in expenditures^2 (in 10,000s)		0.28**	0.21
		(0.10)	(0.14)
Change in expenditures^3 (in 100,000s)			0.12
			(0.21)
σ	10.10	10.01	10.02
R^2	0.09	0.11	0.11
F	10.15	9.88	8.28
DF	4 and 387	5 and 386	6 and 385
N	392	392	392

** $= p < .01$

Conclusion

Overall, the analyses presented in this chapter provide support for the Hovey hypothesis: Higher education does appear to be a balance wheel for state finance. Higher education is cut more than other major spending categories in bad times and receives larger increases than other categories in good times. We also found that the cuts in bad times are larger than the increases in good times for higher education. In addition, we found that the balance wheel hypothesis does not hold for other budget categories.

Given the stability of the balance wheel model over the 1990s, we think there is predictive power in our findings. We believe that our results are most helpful in changing the way policymakers and higher education leaders view the process of state funding for higher education. As we have shown, volatility is the norm in the budgeting process. Higher education

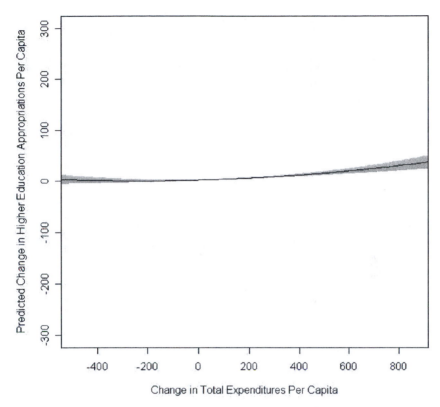

Figure 3.5 Simulated Change in Spending on Corrections by Change in Total State Spending.
Source: Table 3.6, Model 2. All other variables held at mean.

should expect to be treated as a balance wheel during state budgeting processes.

Given the prevalence of volatility, we think that year-to-year changes are important and deserve more study in the field, both in comparative-state studies and within-state analyses. In particular, we urge researchers conducting cross-state studies to take the idea of studying change more seriously than has been done in the past. The vast majority of state-by-state studies are essentially static in nature. These studies look at the absolute levels of state appropriations, tuition, or financial aid as a function of state characteristics. Even studies that make use of panel data use models that rely on absolute levels of various state higher education policy outputs. We suggest that year-to-year changes should be studied more closely.

Knowing how higher education is treated in state budgets can also allow for more nuanced discussions among legislators and higher education leaders about how best to preserve the public good created through higher education. When states face hard economic times, legislators are likely to look to higher education for budget cuts. Since tuition increases are frequently the institutional response to reductions in appropriations, tuition increases happen at the moment when students and families are least able to pay for college—when the economy is bad and savings have lost value. From the perspective of legislators there are incentives to reduce the volatility of budgeting for higher education to help ensure that access is not cut off for students. From the higher education perspective, stability in state appropriations is also attractive for more accurate budgeting and to reduce surprise tuition increases for their students.

Given the mutual benefit of reducing the volatility of state appropriations for higher education and our sense that our findings will hold true in the future—that higher education will continue to serve as a balance wheel—we offer two recommendations. First, allow public universities to build rainy-day funds. If institutions are able to build reserves during good times, then they can use these funds during bad times and mitigate potential tuition increases. Second, include discussions of stability (in addition to increases in funding) in annual negotiations of state appropriations for higher education. Of course, stability cuts both ways—asking for smaller cuts in bad times means asking for smaller increases in good times. We believe that the increased ability to plan for the future and to make long-range strategic decisions would be worth the trade-offs inherent in such a deal.

Notes

1. Although it is an interesting topic, exploring the causes of the balance wheel in detail is beyond the scope of this chapter. Please see Hovey (1999) for a more detailed discussion.
2. We recognize that there are two other quadrants (upper left and lower right) in figure 3.1, which are left out in this analysis. In our view, these quadrants do not represent categorizations for budget years but rather indicate a shift of budgeting priorities. Thus, for the purposes of this analysis, we focus our attention on the upper right and lower left quadrants.
3. Data are available directly from the Census Bureau only for the years in this study.
4. We fit higher order models to the data, including models that incorporated a quartic and a quintic functional form. The quartic model resulted in estimates that slightly improved model fit, whereas the quintic model did not significantly increase model fit. We found only a slight improvement in the model fit

of the quartic function. The quartic form that best fits the data has an *S* shape that most resembles the balance wheel; hence, we still find general support for Hovey's hypothesis. In addition, because the fourth dimension is not easily defined in the budgeting process, we assume that the increase in fit is a result of the difficulty of modeling budgeting processes and is not an indication that the cubic form does not best describe the data. We hope in future work to be able to use more nuanced data to better model budgeting processes. Because our hypothesis only extends to the functional form of the cubic model, we do not report results for these higher-order models in this chapter. Results from our tests of higher-order functions are available from the authors by request.

References

Betts, J. R., & McFarland, L. L. (1995). Safe port in a storm: The impact of labor market conditions on community college enrollments. *The Journal of Human Resources, 30*(4), 741–765.

Center for Higher Education and Educational Finance. (2002). *Grapevine: A national database of tax support for higher education: Technical report*. Normal: Illinois State University.

Clinton, J., Jackman, S., & Rivers, D. (2004). The statistical analysis of roll call data. *American Political Science Review, 96*, 355–370.

Downs, A. (1957). *An economic theory of democracy*. New York: Harper.

Hovey, H. A. (1999). *State spending for higher education in the next decade: The battle to sustain current support*. San Jose: California State Policy Research, Inc.

Humphreys, B. R. (2000). Do business cycles affect state appropriations to higher education? *Southern Economic Journal, 67*(2), 398–413.

Kane, T. J., Orszag, P. R., & Gunter, D. L. (2003). *State fiscal constraints and higher education spending: The role of Medicaid and the business cycle*. Washington, DC: Brookings Institution.

National Association of State Budget Officers. (2005). *2004 state expenditure report*. Washington, DC: Author.

Nelson, M. (2000). Electoral cycles and the politics of state tax policy. *Public Finance Review, 28*(6), 540–560.

Nordhaus, W. (1975). The political business cycle. *The Review of Economic Studies, 42*(2), 169–190.

Okudade, A. A. (2004). What factors influence state appropriations for public higher education in the United States? *Journal of Education Finance, 30*(2), 123–138.

Rogoff, K. (1990). Equilibrium political budget cycles. *The American Economic Review, 80*(1), 21–36.

Selingo, J. (2003, February 28). The disappearing state in public higher education. *The Chronicle of Higher Education*, p. A22.

Toutkoushian, R. K., & Hollis, P. (1998). Using panel data to examine legislative demand for higher education. *Education Economics, 6*(2), 141–157.

United States Department of Commerce, Bureau of the Census. (2002). *Census of state and local governments.* Washington, DC: Author.

United States Department of Commerce, Bureau of the Census. (2003). *Current population survey.* Washington, DC: Author.

United States Department of Education. (2001). *Digest of education statistics 2000.* Washington, DC: Author.

United States Department of Labor, Bureau of Labor Statistics. (2003). *Employment status of the civilian population by sex and age.* Washington, DC: Author.

United States Department of Labor, Bureau of Labor Statistics. (2004). *Consumer price index for all urban consumers.* Washington, DC: Author.

Wooldridge, J. (2003). *On the robustness of fixed effects and related estimators in correlated random coefficient panel data models.* London: Institute for Fiscal Studies.

CHAPTER 4

Tracking How Ideas Become Higher Education Policy and Practice

The Challenges of Gathering Comparative State Policy Implementation Data

Sara Goldrick-Rab and Kathleen M. Shaw

The implementation process is an increasingly important component of public policy research. The growing trends of devolution and de-bureaucratization mean that it is rare for contemporary written policy to be neatly and linearly translated into practice. This is especially true in the higher education arena, where policymaking often occurs in a decentralized manner and policy implementation is carried out by a set of actors that can be nearly fully disconnected from the policymakers. In such cases, the ideas that drive higher education policy are often not ideas with which higher education practitioners are actively engaged. In other words, the ideology and political beliefs underlying the development of public policy might not be shared among those who are responsible for implementation.

Yet traditional policy analyses in higher education often neglect the implementation process, leaving the reader with the incorrect impression that the relationship between formal policy development and policy enactment in postsecondary education is relatively straightforward. Moreover, many such studies tend to ignore how shifts in ideas lead to changes in public policy. As a result, powerful forces such as cultural and institutional belief systems at both the macro- and micro-levels, which help to determine the degree to which policy developed at a federal or state level is enacted at the local level, are often ignored (Hasenfeld, 2002). In order

Note: The authors wish to thank our collaborators on this study, Christopher Mazzeo and Jerry A. Jacobs, who contributed a great deal to our thinking about this chapter.

to better account for the importance of idea and belief systems and how they affect policy implementation, higher education researchers would benefit from adopting a more comprehensive model of policy research. In particular, we argue that an emphasis on the diffusion of ideas in the policy implementation process is needed in order to fully understand how and why formal policy at the state level varies from enacted policy at the local or institutional level.

An extensive body of literature on policy implementation has developed since the publication of Pressman and Wildavsky's *Implementation* in 1973. Much of this work is concentrated in the arena of public services such as health care, the criminal justice system, and K–12 education. Implementation research in higher education remains largely disconnected from this literature. As Gornitzka, Kyvik, and Stensaker (2002) explicitly point out in the *Higher Education: Handbook of Theory and Research*, policy implementation in the arena of higher education merits substantial attention. Policies emerging at both the state and federal levels (e.g., policies regarding financial aid, affirmative action, and resource allocation, to name a few) have direct impact on this country's colleges and universities, and yet we know little about how such policies are diffused across states and into institutions.

There are, however, some good reasons for the relative lack of attention to policy implementation in the realm of higher education. First and foremost, higher education policymaking is decentralized, and relationships between state governments and higher education institutions are complex (Gornitzka et al., 2002). As a result, policy implementation research is difficult and time consuming. A wide array of data collected from multiple sources and levels of analysis is necessary to develop a thorough understanding of the policy implementation process. Moreover, the real variation that occurs across states makes it particularly difficult to conduct meaningful cross-state comparative analyses. And finally, although there is clear evidence that amorphous factors such as ideas and culture have an enormous effect on policy implementation (Campbell, 2002), they are notoriously difficult to operationalize and study in a consistent manner.

What are the parameters of a study that can successfully analyze higher education policy implementation across multiple states? This chapter focuses on the difficulties inherent in developing a database that is sufficient to arrive at an in-depth understanding of higher education policy ideology and implementation across states. Our arguments are based on a project that examined how two pieces of federal legislation directly affecting higher education—welfare reform and the Workforce Investment Act—were implemented across six diverse state contexts

(Shaw, Goldrick-Rab, Mazzeo, & Jacobs, 2006). Using an array of quantitative and qualitative data, we provide examples of both the challenges and the opportunities in conducting cross-state comparisons of policy implementation. We focus in particular on the difficulties in tracking the development and dissemination of the ideas undergirding policies at the federal level and documenting how such ideas are either enacted or resisted at the state and local levels.

The Importance of Ideas in Policy Implementation Research

As noted earlier, in recent years a diverse and rich body of literature has emerged across the social sciences on the role of ideas in public policy-making (Campbell, 2002; Goldstein, 1993; Goldstein & Keohane, 1993; Hall, 1993, 1997; Kingdon, 1984; Somers & Block, 2005; Weir, 1992, 1993). Research on ideas provides a more nuanced alternative to interest-based explanations of political and social phenomena. As recent scholarship has shown, policy ideas, once institutionalized, can strongly influence the behavior of policy actors (see Hasenfeld, 2002; Lin, 2000; Maynard-Moody, 2003; Spillane, Reiser, & Reimer, 2002; Stein, 2001, 2004).

Ideas assert their power over policy implementation via two major institutionalization mechanisms. The first mechanism is through law and incentives (Goldstein, 1993; Pierson, 1993; Weir, 1992; Weir & Skocpol, 1985; Weiss, 1990). Policy ideas are generally enacted through legislative processes and formalized through statute and legal interpretation. Statutory law creates rights and obligation and builds in a set of formal rules that govern the behavior of state and local implementing agencies. Implementers will not always comply with rules, of course, but laws create powerful incentives to do so, even for those who do not believe in the ideas (Goldstein & Keohane, 1993). In short, when policy ideas become laws, they change the interest calculations of those who must implement them.

Policy ideas can also become institutionalized through their role as focal points or signals (Garrett & Weingast, 1993). Ideas are powerful political forces because they can cause people to think and act differently (Spillane, 2004; Spillane et al., 2002). Political actors and policy entrepreneurs are aware of this and seek to frame policy ideas in ways that are marketable and resonant with other politicians and the general public. Policy ideas that are adopted widely are thus likely to be those that are easily understandable, simple to describe, and commanding of broad support.

Ideas are powerful players in higher education policy as well. But the process of implementation and the transmission of ideas are far less visible in postsecondary research in comparison to studies of policy outcomes (Gornitzka et al., 2002). Higher education would do well to consider the importance of ideas in policy enactment, particularly because "the study of policy and politics" is said to be "quickly becoming a central subfield in higher education" (Bastedo, forthcoming, p. 1).

One realm of higher education research that explicitly acknowledges the role of ideas in policy is that of race, class, and gender studies. For example, Shaw's (2004) analysis of welfare policy identifies the complex ways in which that policy was gendered both in its framing and its outcomes. The framing of policy ideas is crucial to their success—indeed they are more widely accepted when framed as race and gender neutral (Shaw, 2004). Slaughter and Rhoades (2005) examine how capitalism has become hegemonic in defining the worth of higher education as a private rather than a public good. And shifting definitions of concepts such as *merit* and *diversity* drive recent policy debates regarding financial aid (Heller, 2002) and affirmative action (Gurin, Dey, Hurtado & Gurin, 2002).

Ideas have also played an important role in studies of policy adoption in higher education, for example, in the classic study by Hearn and Griswold (1994), which examined the impact of economic and governmental influences on policy innovation. In more recent research McLendon, Heller, and Young (2005) examine the importance of political processes and in particular the interstate migration of policy ideas. They find these to be especially strong predictors of policy adoption—in other words, the philosophies and ideas present in policies appear to exert an effect on the likelihood of policy adoption by acting as policy "signals" to important actors. The authors note that their findings in this area are tentative and deserve greater exploration, because "scholars largely have ignored systematic investigation of the impact of state political institutions and processes on postsecondary policy patterns" (p. 387).

Most examples of how implementation processes can be made central to higher education policy study are found in comparative higher education studies in Europe, such as a study of the implementation of European higher education reform initiatives (Cerych & Sabatier, 1986) and a study of French higher education (Musselin, 2000). Yet as a body of literature, studies of implementation in higher education policy research are incredibly rare. As Gornitzka and his colleagues (2002) note, when searching the higher education literature, "It is not an easy task to find studies that carry the word 'implementation' or a reasonable synonym in the title" (p. 401).

The literature on K–12 schooling provides some examples of how informative studies of policy implementation can be. For example, Linda McNeil's (2000) *Contradictions of School Reform* is an excellent, close-up study of how standardized testing affects the workings of poor urban schools. McNeil's analysis clearly demonstrates how a policy can have both intended and unintended consequences when implemented. In *The Education Gospel*, Grubb and Lazerson (2004) identify the strong role that ideology has played in vocational education at both the secondary and postsecondary levels. In highlighting the power of rhetoric, the authors manage to shed some new light on an old debate in higher education policy.

Despite the merits of these studies, too few provide us with the scope or variety of data needed to construct detailed portraits of how policy implementation processes work. Indeed, of the existing body of implementation studies in higher education, the vast majority employ only one methodology—either focusing on quantitative outcomes, or using qualitative data to describe the implementation process and only speculate at outcomes. As a result, we are left without a methodological approach to constructing a study that will provide enough detail about either policy outcomes, or the implementation processes that lead to them.

Constructing a Comparative Higher Education Policy Implementation Study Framework

Although there has been some discussion in recent years about the methodological weaknesses of higher education research and where improvements might be made (for example, see Kezar & Talburt, 2004), these discussions often neglect the study of higher education *policy*. One exception is a forthcoming chapter by Michael Bastedo (forthcoming), which notes the need for more research methodologies in higher education policy, in particular qualitative research crossing multiple qualitative levels of analysis.

In order to illustrate the comprehensive nature of a database that would allow cross-state comparisons of policy implementation, we draw on lessons learned from a study in which we (along with our colleagues Jerry A. Jacobs & Christopher Mazzeo) examined the complex ways in which welfare reform affected college access in six states. Although it is a federal policy, the Personal Responsibility and Work Opportunity Reconciliation Act (PRWORA) of 1996 emerged in a context of "devolution," in which states received a relatively high degree of autonomy in responding to federal legislation in exchange for meeting relatively strict performance measures. As a result of this policy context, states have the potential to vary considerably in terms of their response. Because of these factors, we felt that it was important to closely compare the implementation of welfare reform across several states.

Our central concern was developing an understanding of how and why college access for the poor had changed under welfare reform. As our data collection and analysis process unfolded, we became increasingly interested in the power of the idea central to the policy, known as "work-first"—the notion that putting poor people directly to work would most effectively lead them out of poverty. This idea effectively bypasses education and training, ignoring the potential of increasing human capital. As we illustrate in what follows, the fact that we painstakingly collected so much data from so many different sources allowed us both to identify the work-first idea as the driving force behind policy implementation in the states and to document as well that the idea was so powerful that it could trump formal state-level policy, resulting in a remarkably uniform adoption of work-first practices regardless of whether a state formally adopted this approach to welfare reform.

Sample Selection—Maximizing Variation in State Response to Federal Welfare Policy

When conducting cross-state higher education policy implementation, the issue of sampling is of utmost importance, because our ability to generalize and to see broad patterns across different contexts is critical. In selecting the six states we used in the study, we sought to assemble a sample that varied in terms of general approaches to welfare reform and the level and quality of access to postsecondary education afforded welfare recipients. We also wanted to achieve some level of geographical diversity as well. The six states chosen were Florida, Illinois, Massachusetts, Pennsylvania, Rhode Island, and Washington. Although each state's approach to welfare reform is quite complex, it was possible to place them initially into broad categories based on the amount of access to postsecondary education that is allowed in the state's formal welfare policies (table 4.1). Overall, the six states appeared to represent a broad range of responses to welfare reform and provided a rich and fertile field from which to conduct our analyses.

Developing a Framework for Data Collection

To begin, we used a nested comparative case study design, which is based on the methodology outlined by Charles Ragin, Howard Becker, and others (Ragin, 1987; Ragin & Becker, 1992) that explores ways in which comparative case studies can be used to examine complex social phenomena.

Table 4.1   State Welfare Reform: Formal Policy Regarding Access to Postsecondary Education and Training

State	Access to Postsecondary Education Under TANF
Massachusetts	College attendance without work requirement is not allowed. Recipients must work 20 hours a week while attending college. But many recipients are exempt from this requirement.
Washington	Recipients may attend college for 12 months without work requirement, but only vocational education is allowed. May attend college only if mandated job search fails.
Florida	State has 48-month lifetime limit. Recipients may attend college for 12 months without work requirement and in some instances continue past this point.
Pennsylvania	Recipients must conduct job search. If unsuccessful, they may attend college for 24 months without a work requirement.
Rhode Island	State adopted a human capital approach to welfare reform. Recipients may attend college for 24 months without a work requirement. May continue full-time postsecondary education if necessary after this point.
Illinois	Recipients may attend college full time for 36 months without a work requirement. To continue after that time, they must work 29 hours per week. State uses Maintenance of Effort funds to "stop the clock" for recipients pursuing postsecondary education.

Source: Drawn from data provided by Greenberg, Strawn, & Plimpton, 2000.

We strived to develop a pool of data that would allow us to do meaningful comparisons of the effects of welfare reform across different state and institutional contexts and to identify the factors affecting the implementation of the policies. This approach is in keeping with the recommendations of the Urban Institute's *Assessing the New Federalism Project,* which suggests that variation within and across states resulting from devolution requires intensive, detailed case study analysis (Bell, 1999).

Qualitative data were collected at several different levels. First, we interviewed more than 100 state-level officials in relevant departments (e.g., Education, Human Services, Employment, and Training) and analyzed formal policy development and implementation using existing policy documents and policy analyses provided by a number of policy research organizations as well as the state agencies themselves.

Next, we identified one to three community colleges in each of the six states. These community colleges varied in terms of size and location (urban vs. rural), but we chose institutions that had historically served a significant number of low-income students, including welfare recipients. In this way, we hoped to be able to gauge the effects of welfare reform among community colleges that were most likely to be impacted by shifts in these policies. We interviewed a total of 96 faculty members and administrators at 13 different colleges. We also conducted 11 individual interviews and 4 focus groups of low-income workers. Finally, we interviewed 13 welfare caseworkers. Our interviews were detailed, following a topical script rather than a survey instrument, and often lasted an hour or more.

We also visited each state multiple times over the course of a two-year data collection period (2001–2003) and conducted numerous follow-up interviews as our analysis proceeded through 2005. This extended period of time in the field allowed us to analyze the implementation of both policies over time.

All interviews were tape-recorded and transcribed. We used Hyperresearch, a qualitative data analysis software, to code and analyze the interviews. As is true in most qualitative research, our analytic framework became increasingly specified as analysis unfolded, focusing more carefully on how conceptions of the work-first idea influenced the implementation of welfare reform as it became clear that there was far less variation in the implementation of these policies than written, state-level policy would suggest. We were also particularly interested in discerning both the intended and unintended effects of these policies as they were implemented at the local and institutional levels.

Additionally, we collected an extensive amount of secondary data regarding the implementation and outcomes of both policies, including reports generated by states, research institutions, advocacy organizations, and community colleges. These data sources were used to verify and expand upon information culled from the interviews and to develop interview protocols as the study unfolded.

We complemented our detailed case studies with original analyses of micro-level quantitative data on postsecondary education enrollment. Specifically, we examined the degree and type of change in postsecondary education participation that occurred in the wake of welfare reform. National analyses of welfare reform and postsecondary activities were conducted using the Current Population Surveys (CPS), the National Household Education Surveys (NHES), the Surveys of Income and Program Participation (SIPP), and the National Postsecondary Student Aid

Studies (NPSAS). In addition, descriptive state-level analyses of enrollment in postsecondary education pre- and post-welfare reform were conducted using data provided by state officials at the relevant departments in each state.

In all, our data drawn from both qualitative and quantitative sources allowed us to paint a detailed and comprehensive picture of how the implementation of welfare reform was affecting access to postsecondary education and training for low-income populations. A framework that includes multiple levels of analysis, as well as cross-state and cross-policy comparisons, provided us with a rare opportunity to trace the process of policy implementation across levels of enactment and connect that process to quantitative outcomes.

Challenges

The process of data collection and analysis just described suggests that our research project was relatively straightforward and simple. But such a picture is deceptive, because it implies that we followed a linear trajectory, using strict rules and guidelines. Instead, our road toward collecting the substantial body of data needed to conduct our analyses was fraught with potholes, twists, and turns—and in some cases major street improvements were needed before we could proceed. The most important of these are described in what follows.

Identifying Consistent and Reliable Data Sources Across States

As noted earlier, it is essential in any study of policy reform to collect data about the outcomes—both intended and unintended—of the policy. Moreover, good studies of policy implementation "analyze and 'follow' a given policy through the implementation process" (Gornitzka et al., 2002, p. 382; see also Pressman & Wildavsky, 1973). In this case, we were particularly interested in assessing one particular outcome of welfare reform and the Workforce Investment Act (WIA): the level of college access among welfare recipients and low-income adults. Yet because the most basic intent of both policies was to reduce caseloads rather than to reduce college-going activity per se, states were not required to collect data on college attendance or retention. As a result, that measure had to come from original data collection across all of our states.

We began that data collection process under the incorrect assumption that the data we required would be available from similar agencies in each state, perhaps the Department of Education or Human Services. How-ever, we found little consistency in this regard. Whereas states with highly centralized data systems such as Florida could locate these numbers rela-tively easily, other state agencies were entirely unable to do so. For exam-ple, in Washington state, we were forced to turn to another source—the community and technical college governing board—in order to get the data. In the end, our data on college going came from a range of sources—welfare agencies, departments of labor, departments of education, and so on.

Ensuring a Common Definition of Key Variables

The data collection process led to our next challenge—making meaning of the terms used across these states and agencies. We realized quite quickly that the term *college* means different things to different people, different agencies, and different states. Was a welfare recipient attending college if she was enrolled in a two-week English proficiency course? Or were only those at four-year institutions truly in college? How about those enrolled in remedial or adult education courses? Moreover, who qualified as a *welfare recipient*—someone currently receiving welfare, or someone who recently cycled off? Operationalizing our terms in the lan-guage used by those we collected data from became increasingly impor-tant. We also took careful note of how various definitions helped to reinforce—or in some cases reflect—ideas about college access for the poor across our states.

Budgeting the Time to Collect Necessary Data

Patience was also crucial. It took more than two years to collect all of the quantitative data needed from our six states and involved more than 150 e-mails and dozens of phone calls. In some cases we were passed from one bureaucrat to another, told by one that the data did not exist, and then told by another that it was on his desk. Combined with our work interviewing in the field, our project lasted four years—a substantial in-vestment of research time for a single book manuscript written by four academics.

Triangulating Data

All of these challenges in collecting cross-state data meant that attention to detail was crucial, and more importantly we needed to triangulate our evidence. When one agency said data was not collected, we checked the accuracy of that statement with another agency; often, we found that relevant data did, in fact, exist. When a state or agency representative reported that the state used a certain data definition, we checked for accuracy with others in the same state and also compared it to definitions in other states. In this way, we not only helped to ensure the external validity of our data set, but we opened up a conversation on the meaning of college access for the poor across states. We found that state administrators were often keen to learn more about how other states tracked the issue, and we provided that information.

Tracing Policy Implementation at Multiple Levels

In and of itself, quantitative data cannot provide a complete picture of why or how a policy has changed. As others have noted, policy implementation is a highly interactive process, and those interactions must be examined (Gornitzka et al., 2002). Therefore, in order to understand how policy was translated into practice, we had to go into the field and talk to people. But speaking only to policymakers at a single level—for example the state—would have yielded partial and incomplete explanations. Thus, we interviewed a broad range of actors, including state policymakers, policy implementers at the local level, college practitioners, and students. We then examined our evidence and followed up with additional sources, in order to triangulate our evidence across levels.

Conducting six in-depth case studies at multiple levels was an iterative process; as we conducted rounds of data collection and analysis, we refined our research questions as we moved forward. It is not uncommon in the implementation literature to distinguish between a "top-down" versus a "bottom-up" perspective, or what sociologists often refer to as a deductive versus inductive research approach. Gornitzka and his colleagues (2002) discuss this dichotomy and recommend that higher education researchers employ a bottom-up approach that pays special attention to front-line actors. As Cerych and Sabatier (1986) have also argued, Gornitzka and his colleagues note that "Even in a centralized state, higher education is more 'bottom-heavy' than most social sub-systems and certainly more than lower education levels. Policy implementation then becomes very interactive, and implementation analysis becomes a study of the respective interactions" (p. 402). They go on to state, "Higher education policy implementation is increasingly complicated by its ambiguous and multiple goals" (p. 404). Recognizing this, then, our study—as it crossed levels of analysis and particularly focused on tracing how the ideas of policymakers and implementers affected policy implementation—yielded much fruit.

Comparing Formal Policy to Policy Implementation: The Case of Illinois

As noted earlier, the most comprehensive source of data on college access under welfare reform that existed when our study began was a report issued by the Center for Law and Social Policy (CLASP) (Greenberg et al., 2000) that classified levels of access in states according to an analysis of each state's welfare policy as it was written into legislation. According to that report, states varied in the details of their policies regarding access to postsecondary education (see table 4.1). But as table 4.2 shows, CLASP designated four states as having "high" levels of college access (Florida, Illinois, Pennsylvania, Rhode Island), one with a "moderate" level (Massachusetts), and one with low levels of access (Washington). These categorizations were in large part the basis upon which we chose our sample of states.

But as our analysis progressed, it became clear that this initial categorization only reflected the *formal* welfare policy of each state; it did not take into account the ways in which this policy was being interpreted and acted upon during the policy *implementation* process. As a result, as we increasingly focused our attention on the actual implementation of this policy in each state, our categorization of how states reacted to welfare reform represented a significant departure from the initial typology. As table 4.2 shows, our analyses suggest that, in practice, only one state allows a high level of access to college (Rhode Island). Three states provide "moderate" levels of access (Florida, Massachusetts, and Washington); and two states allow very low levels of access (Illinois and

Table 4.2 Categorization of College Access for Welfare Recipients		
High	**Moderate**	**Low**
Using Formal Policy Classifications **Greenberg, Strawn, and Plimpton (2000)**		
Florida Illinois Pennsylvania Rhode Island	Massachusetts	Washington
Using Implemented Policy Classifications: **Shaw, Goldrick-Rab, Mazzeo, and Jacobs (2006)**		
Rhode Island	Florida Massachusetts Washington	Illinois Pennsylvania

Pennsylvania). These results are surprising because one of those states—Illinois—is often lauded for having rather liberal education policies for the poor.

A discussion of how we arrived at our decision regarding how to categorize Illinois will illustrate how a research design that traces policy ideas across states and levels of policy implementation can pay off. Of our six states, Illinois adopted legislation that appeared—when taken at face value—to allow the most access to college for welfare recipients among the six states in the study. Illinois's state-level policy encompasses several elements that are clearly intended to reflect a human-capital approach to welfare reform. Not only does the state allow postsecondary education to count toward the welfare work requirement, but it also allows recipients' welfare time clocks to be stopped while they are attending college, as long as they are enrolled in degree-granting programs full time and maintaining a 2.5 grade point average.[1] Based on these liberal formal provisions in Illinois, we might expect to see relatively high rates of college attendance among recipients. Moreover, given the rules of the stop-the-clock provision, it would be reasonable to find recipients in longer-term programs likely to yield higher returns and to see a relatively high caseload as well, because time limits are in essence suspended for those attending college.

Yet the Illinois welfare caseload has dropped steadily and precipitously, from nearly 200,000 just prior to welfare reform to fewer than 16,000 in 2003. As a result, the number of TANF (Temporary Assistance for Needy Families) adults enrolled in postsecondary education began to decline as well and by 2001 had dropped to 11 percent of the number enrolled immediately prior to welfare reform. Yet a 1999–2000 survey of more than one thousand Illinois welfare recipients, conducted as part of the Illinois Families Study, found that 84 percent of respondents reported that they "wanted to pursue education and training," and 40 percent of those respondents who were also college-eligible (meaning they had finished high school) specified that they would like to go to a two-year or four-year college (Sosulski, 2004, p. 10). It is highly unlikely that such high demand waned so dramatically over the period of a few years in order to fully explain participation rates of only 4–5 percent in 2002–2003. Moreover, although the percentage of TANF adults in college with their clocks stopped has increased over time, it has never exceeded 20 percent of the total number of cases. Thus, the formal stop-the-clock provision failed to move more recipients into college, and perhaps more surprisingly, it actually stopped the clock of relatively few who did go. In Illinois, liberal policy did not translate into liberal practice.

Barrier One: The Devil Is in the Details

There are several reasons for this discrepancy. First, one of the most powerful ways in which work-first affects college access is by simply moving more low-income women off the welfare rolls. Although we are not arguing that welfare ought to be the primary mechanism via which low-income adults should access college, it is important to recognize that poor women with young children require more than tuition support in order to attend college. By withdrawing their monthly check, health coverage, and often child care, states make it increasingly unlikely that they will have the time or resources needed to upgrade their skills in postsecondary education. The declining caseloads in Illinois directly contributed to the steep declines in the number of TANF women in college.

A second reason regards the specific rules used to decide whether a recipient's clock would be stopped. As noted earlier, in order for a recipient's aid clock to stop, she must be enrolled full time, have at least a 2.5 GPA, *and* must be in a degree-granting program. These rules raise several problems. First, although recipients are exempted from the work requirement while they attend college in Illinois, they are not exempted from caring for their children, nor are they often provided with child care. Thus, it is quite a struggle for them to enroll full time in school. It is worth noting that part-time attendance is increasingly common not only among welfare recipients but among the college-going population writ large—two-thirds of community college students nationwide attend primarily part time (Berkner, Horn, & Clune, 2000; U.S. Department of Education, 2003).

Third, there are significant class differences in the academic preparation individuals receive throughout their lives, which results in a cumulative disadvantage among our poorest adults. More than 40 percent of the TANF caseload in Illinois lack a high school diploma or GED (Chicago Jobs Council, 2003), which also makes it quite difficult to obtain federal financial aid. As a result, these women, even those with a high school diploma or GED, are unlikely to be adequately prepared for college-level work and are thus less likely to perform well academically during their initial years without significant academic and social support.

Fourth, the requirement that recipients be in a degree-granting program in order to stop the welfare lifetime limit time clock disqualifies many recipients from receiving this benefit, because a) many of these programs require adult basic education and/or a GED and b) the work-first philosophy pushes recipients into shorter-term vocational training. It is thus not surprising to find that among TANF adults in Illinois, the greatest proportion are enrolled in non-degree-granting vocational programs,

ABE, and GED programs, whereas fewer than 3 percent are in degree-granting academic or vocational programs. In other words, taken together, very few welfare recipients in Illinois meet the qualifications to have their clocks stopped while attending college. As a result, barely one-fifth of TANF adults enrolled in college in Illinois have had their clocks stopped.

Barrier Two: The Triumph of the Work-First Idea

But there is another, more complex, reason that seemingly liberal changes in welfare policy in Illinois did not translate neatly into practice. Although there were some small increases in college participation among TANF adults and small increases each year in the percent of adults in college with their clocks stopped, overall fewer and fewer low-income women were accessing college as welfare recipients each year. The reason, we contend, is the power of the work-first idea in the implementation of welfare policy.

In brief, not everyone in the welfare administration agrees with the stop-the-clock provision. In the case of Illinois, despite the state's education-friendly legislation, leadership in the Illinois Department of Human Services (IDHS) fully embraced the work-first philosophy of the federal welfare reform in the early years of implementation. Within this department, welfare reform was interpreted as strictly focused on immediate workforce attachment, in spite of the formal change in rules. One informant reported that the director of the department "was single-mindedly driven by work-first and his whole thing was any job is better than no job, and that's what drove everyone there [at IDHS]." Said another advocate, "Although Illinois kept its plan the same plan on paper, what happened [was] that, essentially, very, very few people were allowed into education and training . . . the prevailing philosophy was get a job, any job, and get it quick."

Work-first was a powerful message in Illinois, one that often transcended written policy. Work-first was promoted by administrators at the top of Illinois's welfare reform, and that message was clearly heard by the caseworkers meeting daily with clients across the state. Yet the pro-education stop-the-clock provision was reportedly unpopular with some caseworkers and their supervisors, who failed to inform recipients of these new options. According to one welfare advocate, "these caseworkers I think really embrace the notion of preaching about getting a job . . . they did buy in well ideologically speaking, they support the [work-first] philosophy." He added, "The consistent message they get is caseload reduction, enter employment, and everything else is bullshit. . . . There are a lot of cases of people who said 'I want to go to college' and their work-ers say 'you can't, you need to go to work.' The overall message coming from the top was get people off, get people off, and education didn't fit in." Again we see the power of the caseworkers in the implementation process, as well as a clear example of how informal communications re-garding the work-first message trumped formal policy.

Thus an idea—work-first—clearly played a role in these outcomes, most strikingly in the implementation process. Illinois provides an exam-ple of how powerful an idea can be *despite* policy that contains relatively generous formal human capital provisions. As our interviews clearly show, a relatively liberal welfare reform policy was implemented in a de-cidedly work-first manner. As a result, despite the opportunity for wel-fare recipients to use degree-focused postsecondary education to count as a work requirement—and despite the fact that such enrollment would stop the welfare clock—relatively few have taken advantage of these provisions.

Lessons Learned

This chapter argues that only a multilevel research design crossing both states and levels of policy implementation will yield a nuanced under-standing of the implementation process in higher education policy change. A simple survey designed to assess policy outcomes is unlikely to either capture the outcomes themselves accurately or account for the implementation process. That said, the more complex research process that we engaged in while trying to understand the impact of welfare re-form is a difficult one, and we have learned several lessons from engaging in it.

First, in designing such a study, states should be selected in part based on the availability of relevant state-level data. Relevant state and local agencies should be contacted in advance, and determinations about the quality and the availability of data made. The downside to this form of selection is clearly the risk of selection bias—those states that do collect such data might differ in significant, unobservable ways from those that do not. However, if one is not attempting to make strong causal argu-ments regarding the policy implementation process and instead is fo-cused—as we were—on understanding more qualitatively how and why ideas were translated into practice—selection bias is less of a concern.

Second, it is useful and important for the research team to collabora-tively create definitions of categories for data collection up front, before collection begins. However, these categories should be somewhat flexible, as researchers will have to be amenable to the understandings and realities faced by state officials, who often have to define terms in specific ways owing to legislative or other preferences.

Third, as in all research, attention to detail is essential. Following an idea—in both rhetoric and in practice—as it is interpreted, enacted, and reified, requires close consideration of evidence obtained from interview transcripts and other sources. Further, evidence should be triangulated across policy actors, so as to not privilege one level of policy actor over another in the research process.

Finally, in keeping with the previous lesson, combining the collection of quantitative and qualitative data within a single study is both an enormous challenge and an opportunity. A real sense of policy enactment "on the ground" as it affects peoples' lives will only be obtained by entry into the field, but quantitative data is also needed in order to examine how widespread and effective the policy outcomes are.

We are not the first to point out the need for careful cross-state comparative analyses of policy implementation and ideas in higher education, and we will not likely be the last. Our field is ripe for such research, and we hope that this discussion of the challenges we faced and the lessons we learned will stimulate future studies.

Notes

1. This is an important aspect of the state's policy, because time limits on welfare receipt exert significant pressure on recipients' lives, often affecting their decisions and structuring how they meet the work requirements

References

Bastedo, M. (Forthcoming). Sociological frameworks for higher education policy research. In Gumport, P. J. (Ed.), *The sociology of higher education: Contributions and their contexts.* Baltimore, MD: Johns Hopkins University Press.

Bell, S. (1999). *New federalism and research: Rearranging old methods to study new social policies in the states.* New York: The Urban Institute.

Berkner, L., Horn, L., & Clune, M. (2000). *Descriptive summary of 1995–96 beginning postsecondary students: Three years later* (NCES 2000–154). U.S. Department of Education, National Center for Education Statistics. Washington, DC: U.S. Government Printing Office.

Campbell, John L. (2002). Ideas, politics and public policy. *Annual Review of Sociology, 28,* 21–38.

Cerych, L., & Sabatier, P. (1986). *Great expectations and mixed performance: The implementation of higher education policies in Europe.* Stoke-on-Trent, England: Trentham Books.

Chicago Jobs Council. (2003). *From safety net to self-sufficiency: A CJC proposal for a state mixed strategy approach to prepare TANF and food stamp employment and training participants for Illinois' skilled workforce.* Chicago: Author.

Garrett, G., & Weingast, B. (1993). Ideas, interests and institutions: Constructing the European community's internal market." In Goldstein, J., & Keohane, R. (Eds.), *Ideas and foreign policy: Beliefs, institutions and political change* (pp. 173–206). Ithaca, NY: Cornell University Press.

Goldstein, J. (1993). *Ideas, interests and American trade policy.* Ithaca, NY: Cornell University Press.

Goldstein, J., & Keohane, R. (Eds.). (1993). *Ideas and foreign policy: Beliefs, institutions and political change.* Ithaca, NY: Cornell University Press.

Gornitzka, Å., Kyvik, S., & Stensaker, B. (2002). Implementation analysis in higher education. In Smart, J. C. (Ed.), *Higher education: Handbook of theory and research* (pp. 381–423). Vol. XVII. New York: Agathon Press.

Greenberg, M., Strawn, J., & Plimpton, L. (2000). *State opportunities to provide access to postsecondary education under TANF.* Washington, DC: Center for Law and Social Policy.

Grubb, W. N., & Lazerson, M. (2004). *The education gospel.* Cambridge, MA: Harvard University Press.

Gurin, P., Dey, E., Hurtado, S., & Gurin, G. (2002). Diversity and higher education: Theory and impact on educational outcomes. *Harvard Educational Review, 72*, 3.

Hall, P. (1993, April). Policy paradigms, social learning and the state: The case of economic policy making in Britain. *Comparative Politics,* 275–296.

Hall, P. (1997). The role of interests, institutions and ideas in the comparative political economy of the industrializing nations. In Lichbach, M., & Zuckerman, I. (Eds.), *Comparative politics: Rationality, culture and structure* (pp. 174–207). Cambridge: Cambridge University Press.

Hasenfeld, Y. (2002). *The making of the black box: An organizational perspective on implementing social policies.* Paper presented at the Workshop on Organizations and Social Policy, Chicago, IL.

Hearn, J. C., & Griswold, C. P. (1994). State-level centralization and policy innovation in U.S. postsecondary education. *Educational Evaluation and Policy Analysis, 16*(2), 161–190.

Heller, D. (Ed.). (2002). *Condition of access: Higher education for lower-income students.* Westport, CT: Praeger.

Kezar, A., & Talburt, S. (2004). Introduction: Questions of research and methodology. *Journal of Higher Education, 75*(1), 1–6.

Kingdon, J. (1984). *Agendas, alternatives and public policies.* Boston, MA: Little Brown.

Lin, A. (2000). *Reform in the making: The implementation of social policy in prison.* Princeton, NJ: Princeton University Press.

Maynard-Moody, S. (2003). *Beyond implementation: A sketch of a theory of policy enactment.* Paper presented at the Annual Research Conference of the Association for Public Policy Analysis and Management, Washington, DC.

McLendon, M. K., Heller, D., & Young, S. P. (2005). State postsecondary policy innovation: Politics, competition, and the interstate migration of policy ideas. *The Journal of Higher Education. 76*(4), 363–400.

McNeil, L. (2000). *Contradictions of school reform.* New York: Routledge.

Musselin, C. (2000). *The role of ideas in the emergence of convergent higher education policies in Europe: The case of France.* (Center for European Studies, working paper series #73). Cambridge, MA: Harvard University.

Pierson, P. (1993). When effect becomes cause: Policy feedback and political change. *World Politics, 45*(4), 595–628.

Pressman, J. L., & Wildavsky, A. (1973). *Implementation.* Berkeley: University of California Press.

Ragin, C. (1987). *The comparative method: Moving beyond qualitative and quantitative strategies.* Berkeley: University of California Press.

Ragin, C., & Becker, H. (Eds.). (1992). *What is a case? Exploring the foundations of social inquiry.* New York: Cambridge University Press.

Shaw, K. M. (2004). Using feminist critical policy analysis in the realm of higher education. *Journal of Higher Education, 75*(1), 56–79.

Shaw, K. M., Goldrick-Rab, S., Mazzeo, C., & Jacobs, J. A. (2006). *Putting people to work: How the work first idea eroded college access for the poor.* New York: Russell Sage Foundation.

Slaughter, S., & Rhoades, G. (2005). *Academic capitalism in the new economy.* Baltimore, MD: Johns Hopkins University Press.

Somers, M., & Block, F. (2005). From poverty to perversity: Ideational embeddedness and market liberalism over two centuries of welfare debate. *American Sociological Review 70*(2): 260–287.

Sosulski, M. (2004). *A road to inclusion: A combined-methods analysis of access to post-secondary education for women in the Illinois public aid system.* Doctoral Dissertation. University of Wisconsin–Madison.

Spillane, J. (2004). *Where the rubber meets the road.* Paper presented at the Education Finance Research Consortium (EFRC) Symposium. New York, NY.

Spillane, J., Reiser, B., & Reimer, T. (2002). Policy implementation and cognition: Reframing and refocusing implementation research. *Review of Educational Research, 73*(3), 387–431.

Stein, S. (2001). These are your title 1 students: Policy language in educational practice. *Policy Sciences, 34*(2), 135–156.

Stein, S. (2004). *The culture of education policy.* New York: Teachers College Press.

U.S. Department of Education. (2003). *Digest of education statistics.* National Center for Education Statistics: Washington, DC.

Weir, M. (1992). *Politics and jobs.* Princeton, NJ: Princeton University Press.

Weir, M. (1993). Ideas and the politics of bounded innovation. In Steinmo, S., Thelen, K., & Longstreth, F. (Eds.), *Structuring politics: Historical institutionalism in comparative analysis* (pp. 188–216). New York: Cambridge Press.

Weir, M., & Skocpol, T. (1985). State structures and the possibilities for "Keynesian" responses to the great depression in Sweden, Britain and the United States. In Evans, P., Rueschemeyer, D., & Skocpol, T. (Eds.), *Bringing the state back in* (pp. 107–169). Cambridge: Cambridge University Press.

Weiss, J. (1990). Ideas, inducements and mental health policy. *Policy Studies Journal, 92*, 178–200.

CHAPTER 5

Challenges to Designing Cross-State Measures of State Resources for Higher Education

William R. Doyle

State policymakers routinely find themselves in the frustrating position of being unable to say what, exactly, they are getting for the resources that they provide to systems of higher education in their states. Although institutional leaders are happy to provide policymakers with a list of input measures, such as dollars spent on different activities, characteristics of students, or such things as student-faculty ratio, none of these actually measure the outcomes of higher education within the state.

Measuring Up, the state-by-state report card on higher education, marked one of the first attempts to change this situation (National Center for Public Policy and Higher Education, 2000). *Measuring Up* contains more than 30 indicators of higher education performance divided into 5 categories: preparation, participation, affordability, completion, and benefits. Using the information in *Measuring Up*, state policymakers could form an objective, if limited, view of the performance of their system of higher education.

However, having information on outcomes does not fully answer the question: What are we getting for what we are spending? After the first release of *Measuring Up*, higher education leaders in many states suggested that low performance was related to low state support for higher education. Evidence for this assertion usually took the form of comparisons of funding levels with preselected "peer" institutions or states.

In response to these developments, the National Center undertook the Resources and Performance Project, designed to create a set of common measures for all states to compare the levels of resources available for their system of higher education. This chapter documents some of the issues involved with creating any common state-level metric for measuring spending on higher education. It then describes the set of measures used by the National Center to compare states on the basis of resources.

Background

There is a long history of research tracking the expenditures of higher education. Efforts to standardize and report uniform college costs can be traced to the 1972 Higher Education Amendments and the resulting report of the National Commission on the Financing of Postsecondary Education (Lawrence, 1975). Many notable attempts to capture all of the relevant issues of college costs have been conducted since then, including the cost-escalation studies of Clotfelter and Ehrenberg (Clotfelter, 1996; Ehrenberg, 2000).

Many of these studies have the seemingly simple goal of figuring out how much it costs to accomplish certain functions within higher education. For example, how much does it cost per year to educate an undergraduate student? What is the cost for a graduate student? How much does research cost? As Breneman (2001) points out, "buckets of ink have been spilled in commentary on college costs" (p. 14). The theory behind these efforts has been that a better understanding of the specific allocation of resources on campuses will enable researchers to identify areas where funds are being spent inefficiently or ineffectively. None of the research done so far has been able to accomplish this goal. The complexity of college and university operations makes these questions nearly unanswerable, given the variation that exists across institutional types, disciplines, lower and upper division students, research area, and so on. These complications do not make the establishment of college costs impossible, but they do make it extraordinarily difficult (Brinkman, 1989).

Two aspects of college and university financing in particular make any attempt to establish "true" costs nearly impossible. First, as Breneman points out, undergraduate education, graduate education, and research are jointly produced (Breneman, 2001). This follows from insights in Nerlove's theoretical framework on college costs, which argues that there is no meaningful way to establish how much of a faculty member's time spent on working with a graduate student in research should be allocated to educational or research purposes (Nerlove, 1972).

Even in institutions where joint production does not seem to be occurring (e.g., community colleges) the other issue that makes establishing college costs nearly impossible is fungibility of funding. Education occurs in a variety of settings in colleges, going from classrooms to the library to laboratories. It is not possible to track each student's usage of each type of educational environment in order to arrive at even a rough estimate of the cost of that student's education (McPherson & Schapiro, 1991).

Given that we cannot know with any certainty the true costs of higher education, what can we reasonably set out to know? We can always look at the overall revenues and expenditures of higher education. According to Bowen's (1980) revenue theory of costs, higher education institutions' means of determining their own cost structure depend solely on the revenue available. As Bowen says, "at any given time, the unit cost of higher education is determined by the amount of revenues available for education relative to enrollment" (p. 19).

The background to this research led to the conclusion that a focus on the revenues of institutions of higher education should be the starting point for any attempt to document state-to-state differences in the financing of higher education.

Previous Attempts at Measuring Revenues

There are two long-running series of reports that attempt to document state-to-state differences in funding higher education. The first is the series of reports on state tax appropriations for higher education known as *Grapevine*. The second is the series of reports on indicators of state efforts in financing higher education created by Kent Halstead. Both are discussed in what follows.

Grapevine

The longest established history on the financing of higher education at the state level is contained in the annual Grapevine reports, published since 1961 and currently housed at Illinois State University (e.g., Palmer, 2005, #56). Grapevine annually reports state tax appropriations for higher education in every state. The report contains information collected from each state regarding the appropriations made to individual campuses, statewide higher education boards and commissions, and student financial aid programs. Grapevine has been used in a number of different analyses and forms the basis for one of the measures used in this chapter.

The original author of the Grapevine reports, M. M. Chambers, warned in 1972 about the difficulties of comparing states on the basis of the resources made available to higher education:

> Persons who wish to examine the figures in the present document at great length will find much that is informative regarding comparisons among states and institutions. It is always necessary to keep in mind that

diversities in the practices among the states make such comparisons of only limited usefulness; that the reduction of the nationwide scene to a semblance of uniformity inevitably does some violence to the actual facts at many points. (Chambers, 1972)

These same "diversities in the practices among the states" continue to be problematic, as I will discuss later.

Halstead Reports

Another voluminous literature on higher education finance was produced by Kent Halstead. In addition to the creation of the Higher Education Price Index (HEPI) and other measures of higher education cost inflation, Halstead produced a steady series of reports on higher education financing in the 50 states (Halstead, 1975, 1999). These reports began as a series of publications compiled by the National Center for Higher Education Management Systems for the federal office of Health Education and Welfare and continued through 1998. The State Profiles series drew on a variety of data sources to create measures of state tax capacity, state tax support for higher education, and family (and student) share of total funding.

In these reports Halstead sought to answer a series of questions about state finance of higher education, including: How much *could* the state spend relative to how much *did* the state spend? What were students and families required to pay for public higher education in the state? How did the state balance the relative responsibilities of students and families in financing higher education (Halstead, 1999)?

The Resources and Performance Project undertaken by the National Center for Public Policy and Higher Education sought to answer many of the same questions, albeit with a focus on linking each of the resource measures to an indicator of the outcomes of higher education. This project makes use of many publicly available data sources that have been consistently collected over the past few decades. These include the revenue and expenditure measures collected by the National Center for Education Statistics, along with measures derived from the *Grapevine* studies. The remainder of this chapter will document the attempts to use and build on the findings of these earlier studies.

Measuring Performance

The first set of critical decisions made in the course of this project regarded how to measure performance of higher education in each of the

50 states. The project team faced decisions about whether to measure performance at the state or institution level, and about the scope of the measures to be used. The decisions regarding these performance measures necessarily impacted the types of resource measures that could be considered appropriate to use.

Level of Measures: State vs. Institution

The first issue to be settled was the level of analysis for the performance measures. There can be no argument that there is a large amount of intrastate variation on such things as participation and completion in higher education. However, we sought, for the sake of both clarity and comparability, to limit the level of analysis for performance to the state level only. State policymakers need to know about institutional performance—but first they need to know how their state compares with others. We sought to provide assistance in providing accurate comparative data as a starting point for state policymakers "drilling down" in their own states (Jones & Paulson, 2000).

Second, we also decided not to make use of each of the more than 30 individual indicators that make up the five categories in *Measuring Up*, but instead to focus on the overall scores for each category of performance (National Center for Public Policy and Higher Education, 2000). The grades in *Measuring Up* were designed to reflect the overall performance of the system of higher education in each of the states, whereas the individual indicators form only a small part of the picture for each policy area. Measuring resources against overall performance demonstrates how the state is performing relative to a broad policy area, as opposed to any particular indicator.

Scope of Measures

As mentioned previously, institutions of higher education are involved in the joint production of a number of outcomes: undergraduate education, graduate education and research, among others. Although we are aware that many states place a great deal of emphasis on higher education outcomes related to graduate education and research, it is also the case that many states place little or no emphasis on these goals. In order to meaningfully compare states on the basis of their resources and performance, we limited performance measures to those outcomes for which all states are responsible: preparation for, participation in, and completion of education up through the bachelor's degree. Descriptions of the measures used can be found in table 5.1.

Table 5.1   Description of Indicators of Resources and Performance

	Name	Description
Performance Measures	Preparation	Measures include: percent of 18–24-year-olds completing high school; standardized test scores; course-taking patterns
	Participation	Measures include: percent of 18–24-year-olds attending college, chance for college by age 19, adult participation in higher education
	Completion	Measures include first to second year retention, six year graduation rate, and degree productivity
Resource Measures	K–12 Resources	All spending on public elementary and secondary education divided by average daily attendance
	State and Local Resources	All state tax and non-tax appropriations for higher education (public and private) divided by full-time equivalent enrollment
	Total Resources (Tuition, State and Local)	All institutional revenues (public and private) from state, local, and tuition divided by full-time equivalent enrollment

Source: National Center for Public Policy and Higher Education (2004), author's calculation.

Measuring Resources

With the constraints on performance measures noted previously, a series of decisions about the resource measures to be used had to be made. Many researchers before us have grappled with these same questions. Our answers are not definitive. Instead, we view them as the most promising way currently available to provide information to state policymakers that allow them to make accurate and fair comparisons between their state and others.

Within every resource measure we used, we had to make some broad-based decisions about what counts and what does not. Included in this are whether or not to count dollars that come into the institution in a restricted or unrestricted form, whether to measure costs in terms of units or marginal costs, and whether to adjust the resource measures we use in order to account for state-to-state differences in the cost of living.

Restricted and Unrestricted Resources

The first set of decisions we dealt with had to do with restricted and unrestricted resources. Many in the field of higher education argue that overall revenue measures for institutions of higher education should not include revenues that come in restricted form. By their very definition, restricted revenues cannot be spent on anything but their specific purpose and so do not enter into any institutional conversations about resource allocation. Because institutions cannot make any decisions about these revenues, so the argument goes, they should not be considered part of the calculation when comparing resources and performance.

The researchers involved with the Resource and Performance Project disagreed with this perspective on several fronts. First it seems difficult to argue that restricted revenues could have no impact on performance measures such as participation and completion. Restricted revenues can have a direct impact on institutional educational production by providing for additional funding for graduate education and related research activities, all of which form a part of the general production function. They can also free up unrestricted revenue for these purposes. Although restricted revenues might not in many cases be subject to many of the resource-allocation decisions made by higher education managers, they are none-theless "real money."

Unit vs. Marginal Costs

Another argument commonly made is that per-unit expenditure grossly overestimates the amount it takes to actually fund the unit in question. For instance, looking at revenues per student in a given institution does not give a measure of how much money it takes to educate any particular student. The more appropriate measure, it is suggested, is marginal cost, which looks only at the amount of additional resources it takes to provide an education to each additional student.

Marginal costs are problematic on many fronts. First, using marginal costs involves an implicit production function, which leads to the question: What is the appropriate measure of output? Most of the marginal cost studies that have been done use student credit hours as the output (Lewis & Dundar, 2001). Although seat time is in many ways the only measure that we have of educational activity in higher education institutions, few would argue that it is a sufficient measure of educational outcomes. Second, marginal costs are not useful for cross-organizational comparisons, although unit costs do provide a wealth of information about the comparative overall costs of institutions. For these reasons, we chose not to use marginal measures, but instead make use of "per-unit" costs of higher education within the states.

Adjusting for Cost of Living

One of the most difficult issues in creating cross-state comparisons of state resources for higher education is in accounting for differences in the cost of living across states. As anyone who has lived in different parts of the country (or even the same state) can attest, a dollar can stretch much farther, depending on where you are spending it. Many respondents to some of our earlier efforts suggested that state-to-state variation in revenues for higher education might in fact reflect primarily state-to-state differences in cost of living.

In the end, we decided not to adjust for state-to-state differences in cost of living both for the sake of clarity and for broader reasons. In terms of clarity, it should be pointed out that there is no commonly accepted state-level adjustment for cost of living. Although several efforts have been made, most of these depend on measures of cost of living within major cities in the state, with some additional information included (Berry, Fording, & Hanson, 2000). It seems that intrastate variation in many states is as high as interstate variation, making many of these state-centered measures less than acceptable. The correlations between state-level measures of cost of living and observed levels of higher education revenues are relatively low. And last, we sought to avoid additional complexity whenever possible. For all of these reasons, no adjustments for cost of living were made.

State-to-State Comparisons

Beyond the basics of exactly how to measure resources, we also encountered difficulties in deciding on what basis to compare very different states. These included differences in the mix of institutions across states, differences in emphasis across states, and differences in sources of revenues across states.

Differences in Mix of Institutions

One of the key differences between states is in the mix of differing types of higher education institutions within states. Aggregate resource measures can mask large within-state differences in spending. For instance, estimated per-student spending by community colleges nationally is about $9,183, whereas per-student spending at public four-year institutions stands at about $27,973 (U.S. Department of Education. National Center for Education Statistics, 2004, table 345).[1] A state that is regarded as having a high average level of resources according to the measurements defined by the Resources and Performance project might only have moderate or even low levels of resources at many institutions, such as community colleges or non-research-oriented institutions.

Of particular concern when discussing the mix of institutions is the mix of private and public institutions in the states. The proportion of full-time-equivalent enrollment in private institutions varies from 50 percent in Massachusetts to as low as 5 percent in Wyoming (U.S. Department of Education. National Center for Education Statistics, 2004, table 201). States with more private institutions will by their very nature have higher average tuition costs, as private institutions charge higher tuition rates than their state-supported public counterparts. On the other hand, states with more private institutions will also generally require lower levels of state funding, since private institutions rely on donative resources as well as endowment income in addition to tuition revenue to fund their operations.

These differences in states with large public or large private systems are readily evident in the data we collected. Many of the states with the highest overall revenues are states with large proportions of students enrolled in private institutions. However, many of these same states have quite low levels of support from state and local[2] sources. The difference is accounted for by reliance on tuition revenues and donative resources.

Differences in Emphasis

States might have differing mixes of institutional types because they have differing goals. The set of performance comparisons defined by the National Center in *Measuring Up* does entail a set of goals that all states should, theoretically, have in common. However, these performance measures were never intended to be a comprehensive list of all the goals that state policymakers might be seeking through their institutions of higher education.

Because of the difficulties in assigning funds to different goals, we are left with measures that can look only at aggregate spending levels. These measures are then compared with performance measures as defined by the Report Card project. However, the resulting comparison cannot truly be thought of as a cost-benefit ratio, because the costs might be comprehensively measured but the benefits are not.

Differences in Sources of Revenues

Despite the difficulties in measuring the goals of states, we can with more clarity provide information about the differing revenue sources of state systems of higher education. In particular, in this project we make a particular effort to document the trade-offs inherent in each state between requiring more state funding for higher education as opposed to requiring more family funding.

The Carnegie Foundation in 1972 suggested a system in which state and federal governments provide about two-thirds of direct expenditures on higher education, and students and their families provide the remaining third (Carnegie Commission on Higher Education, 1973). Although we looked only at state funding of higher education, we found that states vary considerably in the relative responsibility placed on students and governments in paying for higher education. In Rhode Island, only 16 percent of funding comes from the state, and 84 percent comes from students, when expressed as a percent of total revenues. By contrast, in Alaska, 22 percent of funding comes from students and 78 percent from the state (see appendix 5.1 for data sources).

These differences can be accounted for in part by the differing roles of public and private institutions in the state, yet these differences do not account for all of the observed variation. In fact, state policymakers have a great deal of influence on the relative responsibilities placed on students and families. In states with large public systems, this influence is most directly felt in the setting of tuition rates at public institutions of higher education. In states with a large private higher education sector, this influence can be felt in terms of the state's use of student aid to help fund those attending private institutions.

Cost Effectiveness: Not There Yet

According to Levin and McEwan (2001), cost-effectiveness analysis "refers to the evaluation of alternatives according to both their costs and their effects with regard to producing some outcome" (p. 10). A true cost-effectiveness analysis will include a comprehensive statement of all costs involved, both direct and indirect. This cost will then be compared with a set outcome, to determine the effectiveness of differing approaches in achieving a certain outcome. As Levin and McEwan point out, this assumes that programs will have similar goals and that a common measure of effectiveness can be used.

As described earlier in this chapter, we believe that we can accurately describe performance on goals that all states share. This does not imply that we can accurately describe the goals that each state might have for higher education. State systems of higher education undertake quite different additional goals, depending on the context of the state and the emphases of institutional and political leaders.

Measures of Performance

As mentioned previously, the measures of performance that are used in this project are the category scores for each state on three performance measures included in *Measuring Up*: preparation, participation, and completion. Table 5.1 describes these performance measures.

The preparation category measures how well young people in the state are prepared to attend higher education institutions. Indicators include the percent of young people with a high school diploma and performance on standardized tests, among others. *Measuring Up* is unique among higher education performance reports in including a category for activities that occur before people enter college. However, any attempt to assess the performance of a state system of higher education must include a measure of how well students are prepared to benefit from that system.

Participation in college is a key goal for state policymakers in every state. The participation category in *Measuring Up* measures three things: the overall participation rate of young people, the continuation rate of those who start as high school freshmen through high school graduation and into college, and the overall participation rates of working-age adults. Participation captures the extent to which all persons in the state are taking advantage of the system of higher education, as well as the immediate transition from high school into college of young people.

Once individuals are enrolled in higher education, the next key step is to complete their educational objectives. The completion category in *Measuring Up* includes measures of first-to-second-year retention, as well as six-year completion rates and the overall productivity of the system of higher education as measured by degrees and certificates produced per 1,000 students enrolled.

It is worth mentioning that we did not include two of the graded categories of performance indicators. The category of affordability is essentially confounded with measures of resources—resource decisions in many states have an accounting relationship with measures of tuition and financial aid. Second, the category of benefits, although directly relevant to the long-term functioning of the state's system of higher education, is not a direct result of institutional management of resources in the short term.

Measures of Resources

We make use of three measures of state resources in our project: expenditures per pupil for elementary and secondary education, state and local resources per full-time-equivalent student, and total resources per full-time-equivalent student. Each resource measure is described in more detail in what follows.

The measure of per-pupil spending on elementary and secondary education is included for the purposes of comparison with performance in the preparation category. This measure includes all local, state, and federal funding for students in public institutions within the state. Table 5.2 displays information about the level of resources available from this category in each state. State resources in this category are mapped in figure 5.1.

To measure the effort of the state in providing resources for higher education, we include a measure of total state and local resources for higher education. This is similar to the *Grapevine* measure of state tax appropriations for higher education, with the exception that we also include non-tax revenues. The most important source of non-tax revenues in recent years has been revenues from lotteries, particularly in states with lottery-funded scholarship programs, like Georgia's HOPE scholarship. State tax and non-tax appropriations are mapped in figure 5.2. The measure of state and local resources for higher education is divided by full-time equivalent (FTE) enrollment in the state, using a measure of FTE that is based on credit hours, not a transformation of full-time and part-time students. For the purposes of this research, we use only undergraduate students enrolled in both public and private institutions in the state. Table 5.3 shows the level of state and local resources available to institutions within each state.

To measure the overall level of resources available for higher education, the project uses a measure that looks at the combined amount of tuition, state, and local resources for higher education. This measure is based on institutional reporting of revenues from various sources through the Integrated Postsecondary Education Data System (IPEDS). Some manipulation of the data was required in order to "crosswalk" information between the differing reporting formats of public and private institutions. This resource measure totals the amount of resources received from tuition and fees, local sources, and state sources, divided by the same FTE

Table 5.2 Resources for K–12 and Performance in Preparation

State	K–12 Resources	Preparation Level	Preparation Index Score
High Resources: 80% + of Top Spending States			
New Jersey	11,793	A	95
New York	11,218	A	93
Connecticut	10,577	A	95
Massachusetts	10,232	A	100
Vermont	9,806	C	79
Rhode Island	9,703	C	78
Alaska	9,563	B	82
Delaware	9,284	C	77
Maine	8,818	B	83
Maryland	8,692	A	92
Michigan	8,653	C	74
Wyoming	8,645	C	77
Wisconsin	8,634	B	88
Pennsylvania	8,537	B	82
Moderate Resources: 60–80% of Top Spending States			
Ohio	8,069	C	78
Illinois	7,956	B	87
New Hampshire	7,935	B	88
West Virginia	7,844	C	79
Nebraska	7,741	B	87
Minnesota	7,736	B	87
Indiana	7,734	C	74
Oregon	7,642	C	73
Virginia	7,496	B	89
California	7,434	C	73
Georgia	7,380	C	76
Kansas	7,339	B	83
Iowa	7,338	B	87
Hawaii	7,306	C	76
Missouri	7,135	B	82
Montana	7,062	B	89
Washington	7,039	B	82
South Carolina	7,017	C	76
Colorado	6,941	A	90
New Mexico	6,882	F	59
Texas	6,771	C	77
North Dakota	6,709	B	84
Louisiana	6,567	F	59

(continues)

Table 5.2   (Continued)

State	K–12 Resources	Preparation Level	Preparation Index Score
Moderate Resources: 60–80% of Top Spending States			
Kentucky	6,523	C	72
North Carolina	6,501	B	83
South Dakota	6,424	B	83
Low Resources: 60% or Less of Top Spending States			
Arkansas	6,276	C	73
Oklahoma	6,229	D	70
Florida	6,213	C	76
Nevada	6,079	D	64
Alabama	6,029	D	62
Idaho	6,011	C	73
Arizona	5,964	D	66
Tennessee	5,959	D	70
Mississippi	5,354	D	68
Utah	4,900	A	94

Source: National Center for Public Policy and Higher Education (2004), author's calculations from 2002 data.

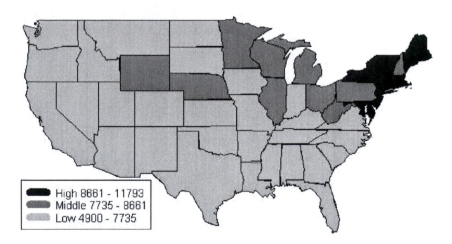

High 8661 - 11793
Middle 7735 - 8661
Low 4900 - 7735

Figure 5.1   Resources for K–12 Education in the United States, 1999.

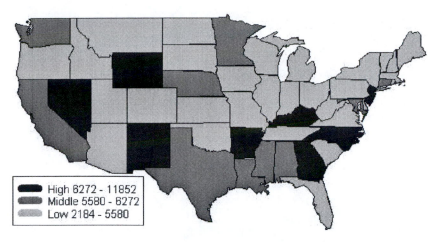

Figure 5.2   State Tax and Non-Tax Appropriations for Higher Education, 1999.

figure as above—these amounts are shown in table 5.3. A map of resource levels in this area is displayed in figure 5.3.

Comparing Resources and Performance

Overall comparisons between resources and performance are detailed in tables 5.2, 5.3, and 5.4. Any number of possible observations could be made, some of which are outside the focus of this chapter. In brief, some descriptive statements about the data include:

Elementary and secondary education spending appears to be quite strongly correlated with performance in participation.
     The relationship between spending and performance is one of the most controversial topics in K–12 education policy. Our work does not shed any light on this debate at the classroom, school, or district levels. Instead, we can only observe that the same states that have high levels of per-student spending are also states that tend to have higher levels of performance in terms of preparing young people for higher education. Figure 5.4 shows performance in preparation plotted against spending.

State and local resources for higher education show tremendous variation, with a maximum of nearly $12,000 in Alaska and a minimum of $2,184 in New Hampshire.
     Differences among states can be seen in figure 5.5. States have designed quite different systems in terms of how much of their own tax

Table 5.3   State and Local Resources and Performance in Participation and Completion

State	State and Local Spending	Participation Level	Participation Index Score	Completion Level	Completion Index Score
High Resources: 80% + of Top Spending States					
Alaska	11,852	C	73	F	53
Wyoming	8,621	B	86	B	89
Hawaii	7,984	B	81	C	75
New Mexico	7,678	A	91	D	66
North Carolina	7,522	C	77	B	86
New Jersey	6,759	A	91	B	83
Georgia	6,542	D	63	B	86
Kentucky	6,484	B	80	C	76
Nevada	6,412	C	76	F	58
Arkansas	6,407	C	71	C	73
Moderate Resources: 60–80% of Top Spending States					
Texas	6,238	C	74	C	73
Mississippi	6,237	D	64	B	82
Alabama	6,234	C	73	B	80
Connecticut	6,196	A	97	B	86
Louisiana	6,139	D	69	C	74
Maryland	6,114	A	93	B	82
California	6,004	A	97	C	74
Nebraska	5,929	A	98	B	84
Washington	5,667	C	74	A	92
Minnesota	5,602	A	96	B	89
Idaho	5,565	C	70	C	77
North Dakota	5,478	A	92	B	84
Florida	5,416	C	75	A	92
Tennessee	5,299	C	71	C	78
Illinois	5,243	A	95	B	86
Delaware	5,237	C	79	B	90
Maine	5,211	B	82	B	85
Oklahoma	5,131	C	74	C	72
Michigan	5,130	B	89	C	79
Kansas	5,076	A	99	B	83
Wisconsin	5,030	B	86	A	91
Virginia	5,016	B	81	B	86
West Virginia	5,004	C	71	C	74

(continues)

State	State and Local Spending	Partici- pation Level	Partici- pation Index Score	Com- pletion Level	Com- pletion Index Score
Table 5.3 (Continued)					
Moderate Resources: 60–80% of Top Spending States					
South Carolina	5,000	C	72	B	85
Indiana	4,993	C	77	B	85
Iowa	4,892	B	89	A	98
Low Resources: 60% or Less of Top Spending States					
Ohio	4,650	C	79	B	84
New York	4,596	C	79	B	89
Utah	4,456	C	77	B	83
South Dakota	4,113	B	89	B	85
Oregon	3,992	C	80	C	74
Pennsylvania	3,875	B	84	A	98
Montana	3,826	C	74	C	76
Missouri	3,622	B	83	B	86
Colorado	3,564	B	86	B	81
Arizona	3,450	B	89	C	79
Massachusetts	2,917	A	100	A	97
Rhode Island	2,749	A	99	A	98
Vermont	2,533	C	73	A	100
New Hampshire	2,184	C	78	A	99

Source: National Center for Public Policy and Higher Education (2004), author's calculations.

resources they devote to higher education. The historical legacy of private institutions in many states is almost certainly related to some of these differences, but policy decisions over time also must play a large role.

The rank-ordering of states according to total resources is quite different than the rank ordering of states according to state and local resources. This indicates that very different sets of states rely primarily on tuition or primarily on state and local revenues.

In general, many Western states rely primarily on public resources, whereas many Northeastern states depend on private resources (see figures 5.2 and 5.3). The extent to which these differing policy stances toward the finance of higher education result in different performance remains unclear. The next section briefly mentions a few techniques that might hold promise in disentangling these relationships.

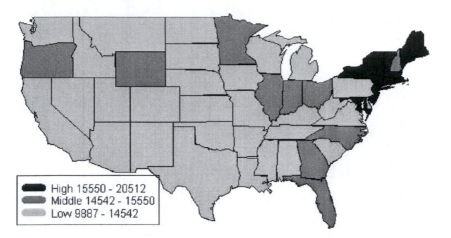

High 15550 - 20512
Middle 14542 - 15550
Low 9887 - 14542

Figure 5.3   Total Resources from State, Local, and Tuition Revenues, 1999.

An Agenda for the Future

This study represents a first effort in this area, one that contains primarily what the Resources and Performance Project members assessed as the appropriate ground rules for making comparisons between resources and performance. In the future, improvements in both data and analyses can be implemented, resulting in richer information available to state policymakers.

First, better data could be collected. Certain types of expenditure data would be enormously helpful. It would be extremely valuable to know how much student financial aid goes to students in public and private institutions of higher education. It would also be quite helpful to have more current data available, particularly from IPEDS, which now has a three- to four-year lag time between data collection and reporting.

Second, more sophisticated analyses are needed in order to answer the question: What are we getting for our dollars? Data envelopment analysis provides one possible approach for analyzing productivity of firms with multiple outputs (Sengupta, 2003). Data envelopment analysis (or DEA) uses linear programming techniques to define an efficiency frontier across multiple outputs. It has been used in other multiple-output settings such as banks and hospitals to determine both the maximum feasible efficiency that units can attain across multiple outputs and the distance for any unit from that frontier. In essence, DEA measures how efficient it is possible for any unit to be and how far any individual unit is from achieving that goal.

Stochastic frontier analysis is another technique for understanding cost effectiveness that is currently being used to analyze the production

Table 5.4 Total Resources and Performance in Participation and Completion

State	Tuition, State and Local Spending	Partici- pation Grade	Partici- pation Index Score	Comple- tion Level	Comple- tion Index Score
High Resources: 80% + of Top Spending States					
Vermont	20,512	C	73	A	100
Massachusetts	19,595	A	100	A	97
Alaska	19,455	C	73	F	53
Connecticut	19,068	A	97	B	86
Rhode Island	18,259	A	99	A	98
New York	17,842	C	79	B	89
Hawaii	17,714	B	81	C	75
Maryland	17,266	A	93	B	82
New Jersey	15,971	A	91	B	83
Maine	15,703	B	82	B	85
Moderate Resources: 60–80% of Top Spending States					
Florida	15,511	C	75	A	92
Georgia	15,312	D	63	B	86
Wyoming	15,121	B	86	B	89
New Hampshire	15,057	C	78	A	99
Minnesota	14,923	A	96	B	89
Indiana	14,861	C	77	B	85
Ohio	14,795	C	79	B	84
Illinois	14,757	A	95	B	86
North Carolina	14,733	C	77	B	86
Oregon	14,575	C	80	C	74
Michigan	14,519	B	89	C	79
Wisconsin	14,061	B	86	A	91
Texas	13,900	C	74	C	73
Washington	13,796	C	74	A	92
Iowa	13,726	B	89	A	98
Nebraska	13,692	A	98	B	84
New Mexico	13,597	A	91	D	66
California	13,511	A	97	C	74
South Carolina	13,372	C	72	B	85
Arizona	12,992	B	89	C	79
Pennsylvania	12,901	B	84	A	98
Missouri	12,867	B	83	B	86
Tennessee	12,817	C	71	C	78
Kentucky	12,742	B	80	C	76
Louisiana	12,427	D	69	C	74

(continues)

Table 5.4	(Continued)				
State	Tuition, State and Local Spending	Partici-pation Grade	Partici-pation Index Score	Comple-tion Level	Comple-tion Index Score
Moderate Resources: 60–80% of Top Spending States					
Virginia	12,186	B	81	B	86
West Virginia	12,139	C	71	C	74
Alabama	12,117	C	73	B	80
Oklahoma	12,053	C	74	C	72
Nevada	12,041	C	76	F	58
Arkansas	11,990	C	71	C	73
Kansas	11,940	A	99	B	83
Mississippi	11,821	D	64	B	82
Low Resources: 60% or Less of Top Spending States					
Colorado	11,292	B	86	B	81
Idaho	11,024	C	70	C	77
Montana	10,726	C	74	C	76
North Dakota	10,429	A	92	B	84
South Dakota	10,358	B	89	B	85
Utah	9,887	C	77	B	83

Source: National Center for Public Policy and Higher Education (2004), author's calculations.

function of schools, with some promise for application to colleges and universities (Coelli & Coelli, 2005). Stochastic frontier analysis uses parametric techniques akin to regression to determine the efficiency frontier for a group of producers. The efficiency frontier denotes the most efficient possible use of inputs that can be realized, given the limits on productivity observed from the data. The results can be used to determine whether any individual producer is achieving maximum productivity, given its current inputs.

Even though measuring aggregate productivity is complex for all of the reasons described in this chapter, it does not mean that it is not a promising area of research. Indeed, the future of state support for higher education might depend on a more refined account of the use of scarce resources for worthwhile purposes.

Appendix 5.1: Definitions and Sources of Data for Resource Measures

K–12 Resources: Unadjusted spending per student. As reported in *Education Week, Quality Counts 2002.*

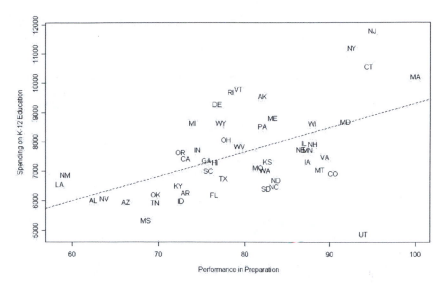

Figure 5.4   Performance in Preparation for Higher Education in Relation to Spending on K–12 Education (2000 data).

Note: The dotted line represents the regression line for the two variables.

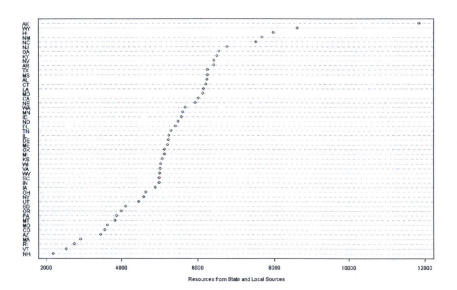

Figure 5.5   Variation in State and Local Resources for Higher Education per Full-Time-Equivalent Student.

Source: U.S. Department of Education, National Center for Education Statistics, "Early Estimates of Public Elementary and Secondary Education Statistics: School Year 2000–2001," February 2001.

State and Local Spending: All state and local tax appropriations for higher education in fiscal year 2001. Figures are reported per full-time-equivalent student.

Source: Center for the Study of Education Policy, Illinois State University. *Grapevine: A National Database of State Tax Support for Higher Education*. Normal: CSEP, 2002. www.coe.ilstu.edu/grapevine/FY01_02.pdf

Tuition, State, and Local Spending: All revenues of institutions of higher education from tuition, state, and local funds. Figures are calculated by sector as follows:

- Public Institutions: All revenues of public higher education from tuition, state grants, state appropriations, local grants, and local appropriations. In addition, revenues directed to administrative units are divided among two-year and four-year institutions according to weights determined by FTE enrollment.
- Private Institutions: All revenues of private institutions of higher education from tuition, state grants, state appropriations, local grants, and local appropriations. Tuition figures are calculated by adding global account revenues from tuition to expenditures for tuition allowances.

Index scores for tuition, state, and local resources are calculated using revenues per full-time-equivalent student for all institutions of higher education. The division of index scores by sector is done by dividing the index score according to the overall amount of resources going to each sector. The division of overall resources is done without reference to student enrollment. Percentages obtained are then used to calculate the amount of the index score apportioned to each sector of institutions.

Source: Full-time-equivalent students; tuition, state, and local resources: U.S. Department of Education, National Center for Education Statistics. *IPEDS Peer Analysis System*. Washington, D.C., 2003. http://nces.ed.gov/ipedspas/

Note: NCES states, "The early release files are provided for peer analysis only, and should not be used to provide aggregate estimates."

Notes

1. These figures were calculated by dividing the total expenditures for the given institutional type by the total number of FTEs enrolled in the institutional type.
2. That is, revenues collected from property and other taxes by counties and other public non-state entities, such as cities or school districts.

References

Berry, W. D., Fording, R. C., & Hanson, R. L. (2000). An annual cost of living index for the American states, 1960–1998. *Journal of Politics, 62*(2), 550–567.

Bowen, H. R. (1980). *The costs of higher education: How much do colleges and universities spend per student and how much should they spend?* (1st ed.). San Francisco: Jossey-Bass Publishers.

Breneman, D. (2001). An essay on college costs. In Carroll, C. D., Cunningham, A. F., Wellman, J. V., Clinedinst, M. E., & Merisotis, J. P. (Eds.), *Study of college costs and prices, 1988–89 to 1997–98* (Vol. 2, pp. 13–20). Washington, DC: National Center for Education Statistics.

Brinkman, P. T. (1989). Instructional costs per student credit hour: Differences by level of instruction. *Journal of Education Finance, 15*, 34–52.

Carnegie Commission on Higher Education. (1973). *Higher education: Who pays? Who benefits? Who should pay? A report and recommendations.* New York: McGraw-Hill.

Chambers, M. M. (1972). *Grapevine: State tax funds for operating expenses of higher education, 1971–72.* Washington, DC: National Association of State Universities and Land Grant Colleges.

Clotfelter, C. T. (1996). *Buying the best: Cost escalation in elite higher education.* Princeton, N.J.: Princeton University Press.

Coelli, T., & Coelli, T. (2005). *An introduction to efficiency and productivity analysis* (2nd ed.). New York: Springer.

Ehrenberg, R. G. (2000). *Tuition rising: Why college costs so much.* Cambridge, MA: Harvard University Press.

Halstead, D. K. (1975). *Higher education prices and price indexes.* Washington, DC: U.S. Dept. of Health, Education, and Welfare, Office of Education.

Halstead, K. (1999). *State profiles: Financing public higher education. 1978 to 1998 trend data.* Washington, DC: Research Associates of Washington.

Jones, D.-P., & Paulson, K. (2000). *Some next steps for states: A follow-up to "Measuring Up 2000." National Center report.* San Jose, CA: National Center for Public Policy and Higher Education.

Lawrence, B. (1975). Cost analysis in postsecondary education: The contextual realities. *Higher Education Management, 3*(1), 1–6.

Levin, H. M., & McEwan, P. J. (2001). *Cost-effectiveness analysis: Methods and applications* (2nd ed.). Thousand Oaks, CA: Sage Publications.

Lewis, D. R., & Dundar, H. (2001). Costs and productivity in higher education: Theory, evidence and policy implications. In Paulsen, M. B., & Smart, J. C.

(Eds.), *The finance of higher education: Theory, research, policy, and practice.* New York: Agathon Press.

McPherson, M. S., & Schapiro, M. O. (1991). *Keeping college affordable: Government and educational opportunity.* Washington, DC: Brookings Institution.

National Center for Public Policy and Higher Education. (2000). *Measuring up 2000: The state by state report card for higher education.* San Jose, CA: Author.

National Center for Public Policy and Higher Education. (2004). *Measuring up 2004: The state by state report card for higher education.* San Jose, CA: Author.

Nerlove, M. (1972). On tuition and the costs of higher education: Prolegomena to a conceptual framework. *Journal of Political Economy,* 80(3), S178–S218.

Palmer, J. C. (Ed.). (2005) Grapevine reports. Normal: Illinois State University, Center for the Study of Education Policy. http://www.grapevine.listu.edu/Welcome.htm

Sengupta, J. (2003). *New efficiency theory: With applications of data envelopment analysis.* Berlin, Germany, and New York: Springer.

U.S. Department of Education. National Center for Education Statistics. (2004). *Digest of education statistics, 2004.* Washington, DC: National Center for Education Statistics.

CHAPTER 6

Developing Public Agendas for Higher Education

Lessons for Comparative Higher Education State Policy

Karen Paulson

Ask not what your state can do for your institution,
but what your institution can do for your state.
—G. Davies

In 2003, the National Collaborative for Higher Education Policy (the Collaborative)—a joint activity of the Education Commission of the States (ECS), the National Center for Public Policy and Higher Education (NCPPHE), and the National Center for Higher Education Management Systems (NCHEMS)—worked with selected states to build on interest generated by *Measuring Up: The National Report Card on Higher Education.* States in the Collaborative included Missouri, Rhode Island, Virginia, Washington, and West Virginia. The Collaborative, with funding from The Pew Charitable Trusts, worked with these states to address problems where need for improvement was indicated by *Measuring Up* grades (Rainwater, 2005). In addition, NCHEMS and its partner organizations have used a similar approach in several other states, including Indiana, Kentucky, Nevada, New Mexico, North Dakota, South Carolina, South Dakota, and Tennessee.

The Collaborative's purpose was to test a single approach—or model—to developing and implementing a state public agenda for higher education. A variety of factors affected how the approach unfolded over time in each state. These factors had to do with which branches of government and which sectors of education had political leadership, whether all institutions in the state operated as peer institutions or a system (whether formally a system or not), the balance of public and private institutions in the state, the demographic mix of the state, as well as whether alumni of the various state institutions held politically powerful offices. Although our work in these states was not in and of itself comparative, there is much to be learned from this project that can inform research by others who are comparing state higher education policy. This chapter outlines some of those lessons and discusses as well the methodological problems that arose when working with states pursuing the development of a public agenda.

Building a Public Agenda for Higher Education

To understand a "public agenda for higher education," we rely on John W. Kingdon (1995) from the public policy arena, who defines *agenda* as:

> the list of subjects or problems to which governmental officials, and people outside of government closely associated with those officials, are paying some serious attention at any given time. (p. 3)

A decade ago few, if any, states could claim that there was a commonly understood, evidence-based agenda—a list of subjects to be addressed— for higher education that guided both institutional and state activities as well as how they all worked together to achieve state-level goals. As state relationships with their public postsecondary institutions have changed over the years, and as budgets have tightened, having a public agenda for higher education has become a way to justify budgetary requests, develop accountability plans that are in keeping with a common agenda, and defend public higher education against budget cuts.

A state's relationship with higher education can be envisioned as two distinct roles. The first, to maintain the assets of higher education, ensures that the state's higher education enterprise has the capacity and quality necessary for the provision of postsecondary teaching, learning, service, and research. The second calls for the state to purchase services provided by higher education specifically for the benefit of citizens and the larger society. The balance of states' attention to these two roles is shifting. Historically states have taken a predominantly institution-centered approach to policymaking, with heavy emphasis on maintaining the existing assets of their higher education systems. More recently, however, states have begun to recognize that they must take a more active role in ensuring that these postsecondary assets are used in ways that address the priority needs of the state and its citizens. These needs are determined by analyzing data from across the state and its regions—a process that is far from straightforward, as I discuss in a later section of this chapter. A lesson for researchers of comparative-state higher education policy would be to always be aware of the extent to which a state's relationship with higher education is guided by "asset maintenance," "purchase of service," or an explicit public agenda.

Higher education is increasingly a central factor in determining the economic well-being and the quality of life in a state and for its citizens. An educated citizenry has become a prerequisite to a competitive economy and a civil society (Carnevale & Desrochers, 2003; Davies, 2004). Although states differ in terms of their specific needs, all depend on higher education's contributions in order to achieve a more desirable future. Increasingly, the role of state policymaking is to forge appropriate links between society's needs and institutional capacity. For example, a state that requires more home health care for an aging population might decide to emphasize community college programs in allied health fields rather than other—perhaps more esoteric or longer-term—initiatives, such as new doctoral degrees at the flagship institution. If states are to attain priority objectives—especially in times of economic constraint—they must invest systematically and wisely in educational programs and activities that have the highest probability of yielding desired results for the state and its citizens.

Building a strong, high-status system of higher education—the purely institution-centered approach of the past—does not necessarily result in production of the services and benefits most needed by the state. Gordon Davies, former state higher education executive officer in Virginia and Kentucky, noted in the course of the Collaborative's work that it is possible, even probable, to have excellent institutions of higher education and still not meet the needs of the state. Unfortunately, very few states have a clear, generally understood sense of priorities. Most do not have a commonly understood agreement regarding the changes that must be made in services to be provided and outcomes achieved if the prosperity and well-being of the state and its citizens are to be ensured. In short, there is no public agenda for higher education in most states.

A key characteristic here is the perspective taken for developing a public agenda for higher education. The question is not whether a state's higher education system is flourishing, but whether the state and its citizens are being well served by the postsecondary capacity (both public and private) available in the state. It is usually true that when a higher education system is not thriving it is also unlikely to be meeting the needs of the state. An example of this situation is Kentucky. Although there is a common misperception that research is not a part of a state's public agenda for higher education, this is not the case. In fact, research is an important aspect of state economic development. When the Commonwealth of Kentucky examined its higher education capacity vis-à-vis a public agenda, it found that the research capabilities of both the University of Kentucky (UK) and the University of Louisville (UL) were not at a level sufficient to best serve Kentuckians. Therefore, an aspect of

Kentucky's implementation of its public agenda for higher education was to support both UK and UL in terms of their research activities that supported the overall needs of Kentucky. However, there are also examples of states with thriving higher education systems that are woefully in need of additional service (for instance, educating adults with high school degrees but no collegiate work) to the state's citizens by postsecondary institutions (for example, North Carolina [see Kelly & Jones, 2005]). Another possible scenario is that a state will have a public agenda with no link to current state needs. California is such a state; it has a long-standing guide to how institutions in the state relate to one another and the state: the Master Plan. This plan is the de facto public agenda for higher education institutions in the state, although one of its weaknesses is that although it explicitly addresses how various sectors of higher education will relate to one another, it does not focus on how the higher education sectors and institutions will work together to meet state needs.

Those analysts comparing state higher education policy will need to be aware that all states differ in terms of the perspective taken toward higher education in a state. Policymakers, institutional leaders, and citizens can view higher education in a state in a number of ways, including to simply see it as a collection of institutions or alternatively as shared capacity to respond to needs of the state.

Activities to Develop a Public Agenda: The Collaborative's Model

The Collaborative's approach to agenda-setting and policy development was generally the same in all of the states participating in the project. It consisted of four primary activities. First, we analyzed data to highlight areas most in need of improvement within the state and regions in the state. Second, we asked state leadership to reflect and comment on issues highlighted by data and to identify those they considered to be within higher education's sphere of influence. Third, we conducted a policy audit to determine which policies affected higher education institutional and individual behaviors with regard to public agenda issues. Finally, states developed action plans based on their public agendas for higher education. Each of these activities provides lessons for comparative policy analysis, and each has its own methodological problems.

Using Data as an Agenda-Setting Tool

The starting point for much of the work with states was *Measuring Up* and the performance of the state on the various categories and subcategories contained in this national report card. *Measuring Up: The National*

Report Card on Higher Education is produced by the National Center for Public Policy and Higher Education (see measuringup.highereducation .org). Using five basic areas—preparation, participation, affordability, completion, and benefits—and available data, *Measuring Up* grades states (based on best-performing states) on how well they do in the five areas. *Measuring Up* grades often serve as a high-profile signal to both legislators and policymakers that a larger issue might exist within the state. For example, legislators might see that the state has a high percentage of the population with baccalaureate degrees (a positive outcome) but that the postsecondary institutions in the state had little to do with educating those people, because they were "imports" into the state (which could be a concern should circumstances change, for instance, if birth or mortality rates change), as is the case in Colorado. Therefore, *Measuring Up* serves as a point of departure, and we perform more fine-grained analyses to get a clearer picture of regional variations within the states, and within subpopulations (e.g., income groups, racial/ethnic groups, etc.). The use of data, however, is rife with methodological issues.

Our experience suggests one lesson learned—and key to any comparison of state higher education policy—is that state-level data can disguise important regional differences within states. For example, sections of Virginia nearest to the nation's capitol are vastly different in terms of wealth and educational levels than the rest of the state of Virginia. Similarly, in New Mexico the population in and near Los Alamos is extremely well educated, an anomaly when compared with the rest of New Mexico. In Rhode Island, the educational attainment level is very different in Providence than it is in the surrounding suburbs. In fact, states are often a collection of loosely affiliated regions, and the differences revealed by disaggregating state averages show that regional needs are often unmet.

Especially when making decisions that will have long-term effects for many people, decision makers want complete and accurate data; in fact, they want perfect data. Unfortunately, perfect databases do not exist at the state level. As a result, very few research studies are available that provide all the data necessary for fully informed guidance on areas in need of improvement. Data that can be brought to bear on issues of particular interest are usually open to challenges of incompleteness and timeliness. For example, census data, which is collected every 10 years, is often criticized as dated when used as the basis for most population and occupational projections done by states and federal agencies. Yet more finely grained and current data at the state level typically does not exist. Other large-scale research (such as the Department of Education's Toolbox and High School and Beyond studies) are rigorous and provide excellent

foundational information; but again, they are open to challenge by policymakers and business leaders who are frustrated because the data cannot
be disaggregated by state and region, and because they, like census data,
are perceived as old.

These concerns—lack of state- or region-specific data and timeliness
of data—lead to two additional methodological problems: satisficing in
the use of data that are available and the need for estimation. Simon (1976)
offered the concept of *satisficing*, which refers to the practice of relying
on available information that is deemed "good enough" to take action,
because an ideal data set is not available. Of course, when working with
states to develop public agendas for higher education we seek to gather
all data available—maximizing the use of all currently available data and
information allows for decisions that are as fully informed as possible at
the time. The bottom line is that state and national databases are imper-
fect; as a result, researchers and policymakers need to do the best with
what is available and adjust expectations accordingly, which leads to the
need to estimate what is happening. And despite data imperfections,
showing policymakers and higher education leaders regional variations is
often revelatory to them.

Despite gathering as much data and information as possible, there are
often questions left unanswered by research studies and available data.
The primary example of this is student progression though the various
levels and sectors of education from kindergarten though graduate school
(as appropriate), known as the educational "pipeline." Many state policymakers desire to focus their efforts in areas of weakness within their states
and within regions in their states. To do so, they want to target resources
at points along the pipeline where difficulties arise. Unfortunately, very
few states adequately follow all their students through the many educational sectors to know where specific problems exist in their states' pipe-
lines. (Note that some states have begun to address the lack of cohort
tracking data through all levels of education problem; Washington and
Florida have focused on it, and Connecticut and Rhode Island have begun
to do initial studies to determine how to address the problem.)

Yet it is still possible to derive relevant information from existing
databases. To help state policymakers understand what is happening, a
variety of estimations may be used. Although percentages calculated from
using a true cohort (all students who entered ninth grade in a single year)
might be unavailable, there are often point percentages available that are
not based on longitudinally following a single cohort of students. For
example, states might know in a particular year how many students who
began as ninth graders actually graduated as seniors from high schools in
the state. And, they might know how many recent high school graduates

attended a public postsecondary institution in the state in the fall after their high school graduation. But these two percentages are not calculated by following the *same* group of students; rather they are based on different sets of students. Nevertheless, these are known percentages. To estimate the effectiveness of a pipeline, these percentages can be applied to a *theoretical* group of incoming ninth graders to illustrate where the largest "leaks" in the pipeline are (NCHEMS, 2003, 2005). The use of estimation is often misunderstood and incorrectly presented as real numbers. Yet, estimation is an important data analysis tool, which is necessary to draw attention to areas in need of intervention in a state or a region. The lesson learned here is to be clear in how state and regional data and information are described and to constantly reevaluate policy and the understanding of that policy in light of new data.

Despite data limitations and methodological issues, we have found when working with states and their stakeholders that these initial data analyses have typically proven sufficiently robust to lead to a preliminary public agenda for a state. This preliminary agenda is a first attempt to describe succinctly the condition of the state and its regions and the areas in which change/improvement are most needed. Perhaps most important, it serves to move the conversation beyond generalities (such as access) to specifics that can be addressed in a meaningful way (e.g., improving access for low-income students in particular regions of the state). For those doing comparative studies of state higher education policy, it would be wise to continually probe for explicit evidence to support suppositions that "everybody knows" in a state. Data analyses result in a more complete understanding of the state and its internal variations based on actual data, rather than assumptions, conventional wisdom, or folklore.

Building a Shared Understanding

The second activity that the Collaborative engaged in when developing a public agenda for higher education in participating states was to work with a leadership group in the state to discuss this preliminary public agenda and to start the process of building a shared understanding about which of the identified issues were the highest priority needs. The leadership group usually comprises educational leaders from across sectors, business leaders, political leaders, and citizens in the state. (Note that "shared understanding" does not mean "consensus" here; rather, it means that everyone has seen the same data and analyses, agreed on the issues facing the state and its citizens, and agreed to move forward—not that everyone agrees on the specifics of how change will be achieved.) It is at this point that a set of additional barriers to agenda-setting emerges.

The first methodological problem is the political culture of a state. Taking the first step toward creating a public agenda for higher education is nearly impossible without someone in the state willing to put her or his personal political capital at risk. The person who does this can be from any number of roles: governor, legislator, business leader, and so forth. The reasons these individuals step forward vary from state to state; in some cases they are newly elected and want to affect a reform agenda. In others, they can be near retirement and want to leave a lasting mark, and in still other cases, they can be well-respected individuals who understand that the time has arrived for leadership in this area. In any case, someone in a leadership position in a state must want—and be able to—carry the message of the public agenda for higher education vigilantly and consistently. In recent public agenda-setting activities in Kentucky and Virginia, the governor at the time was the primary leader; in West Virginia the chair of the Senate Education Committee led the process. In Rhode Island it was a combination of business leaders, the state higher education executive officer, and the chief state school officer; and the governor led each meeting.

The corollary to the need for leadership at the beginning of the process and the second methodological problem is the need for leadership *across time*; that is, leadership of the public agenda across transitions in political leadership. The need for leadership across time arises because adopting an agenda does not result in immediate change. Implementing a public agenda for higher education can fall victim to election cycles, economic downturns, term limits, diffusion of focus, and so on. One method for tempering these effects is to use a "roundtable" with membership from areas previously noted (education, business, political) that crosses political and election cycles and is refreshed with new members over time. By doing so, seasoned roundtable members can offset desires of new members to change direction or move attention off the agreed-upon public agenda for higher education. A mechanism for periodic (at least annual) leadership group review of the priorities, progress that has been made, and any new policy initiatives is an absolute necessity. This process is also important as a device for orienting new members of the policy group, a requirement if the agenda is to stay in effect long enough to make a difference. North Dakota has been quite successful with its roundtable, as has been South Dakota. But, these two adjacent states have taken different approaches to the same idea. South Dakota's roundtable is a project of the state higher education executive officer, whereas North Dakota's is driven by the legislature. In both cases, however, the roundtables bring multiple stakeholders into the conversation about how higher education participates in the state's interest.

Comparative policy analyses should be framed with a clear understanding of who the real and political leaders in the state are as well as how external circumstances (an election or judicial ruling) can either end or substantially slow forward movement on a public agenda for higher education in a state.

The Policy Audit

The third activity in moving forward on a public agenda for higher education is the conduction of a policy audit—that is, an assessment of the policies currently in place and a determination of the extent to which they contribute (or serve as barriers) to addressing the identified priority needs. Higher education institutions operate within a complex environment of policies and procedures that have accumulated over time. Many enacted policies address issues that might now be long forgotten but still shape institutional behavior. These policies and procedures yield the results that might now be deemed unsatisfactory in specific areas and in need of change. For instance, in some states funding mechanisms continue to reward student enrollment rather than successful completion. Existing policies might actually mitigate against dual enrollment programs, because in some states these students can only be counted by one educational sector—either the high school or the community college—but not both. Another example is adult literacy, which in many states has historically been associated with workforce development rather than education units; the result is that there is little or no governance or policy in place to address how to integrate adult literacy (which can account for a substantial portion of the adult population in a state) with state needs and postsecondary education. Therefore, before adding new policies, programs, or procedures to those already in place, an audit of the current array of policies is needed.

The objective of conducting a policy audit is to remove barriers—both real and perceived—that would continue to be impediments even if the state and its postsecondary institutions enacted well-designed new policies. The policy audit accomplishes three outcomes. It provides evidence of whether policies are aligned with one another and with the public agenda for higher education. It highlights whether policies are balanced with regard to the public agenda for higher education. And, a policy audit uncovers whether policies are regularly reviewed to maintain their alignment and balance with one another and with the public agenda.

A policy audit can be conducted by individuals external to the state, by a cross-section of people from within the state, or by a combination of both. It is best to include individuals with a fresh perspective in the policy audit. Internal state people from the group spearheading the public agenda work, whether it is the state higher education executive agency, a legislative committee, or a business group, can conduct the policy audit. Policy audits of some scope—limited to full-blown—have been conducted in all of the Collaborative states; and NCHEMS regularly does policy audits for both states and institutions. For example, as a result of a policy audit, community colleges in Kentucky are no longer structurally part of the University of Kentucky; and in Louisiana the community and technical college system is being restructured into regional service entities in response to a policy audit. Another example is that the state of Washington is currently taking steps to improve policy linked to adult education, including funding.

Methodological issues that surface during policy audits include the difference between real and perceived policies and the need for multiple perspectives on policies (e.g., not just academics, but also business leaders, community members, etc.). In addition, methodologically it is necessary to discern at what level policies need to be addressed—state, system, or the individual institution level. The lesson learned here for comparative higher education policy is that each state is unique; therefore, successful policy development and implementation requires an analysis of why the current system and policies are in place. Doing so allows researchers and policymakers to identify the multiple factors that can influence targeted policy areas.

The issue of real versus perceived policies is not a trivial one. Many times in our work we have discovered that behaviors have been built on a perceived understanding of what a policy says. Upon further investigation, we find that the policy is not stated as everyone assumes and perceives it to be and that many years of practices have been built on incorrect readings of or interpretations of what the policy was meant to do. Unraveling both the real and perceived policies and practices can take concerted effort over time to clarify what is happening. There can be considerable confusion regarding what is actually a policy or in statute and what has just been traditional practice ("we've always done it that way"). For example, it is not unusual for state policymakers to inaccurately believe that standing procedures are the result of actual policy, when in fact they are not. Three examples are 1) the role of part-time non-credit instruction in funding formulae, 2) the type of students (full-time or part-time or both) that are allowed to participate in various financial aid programs, and 3) whether states pay for workforce development instruction. The key learning here for those comparing state higher education policy is to be aware of the possibility of perceived policies interfering with actual policies.

Multiple perspectives on these issues are necessary because in the past, policy discussions have often erred on the side of asking only for the perspective of colleges and universities in the state. For example, rather than examining the postsecondary needs of the entire population of a state, the default until recent years has been to develop policy based on data drawn only from the pool of individuals who have already enrolled in postsecondary institutions. Unfortunately, this method underestimates the educational needs of a state, because the entire population of the state is not accounted for—only that population that had self-selected through a variety of mechanisms to pursue higher education at an institution in the state was selected. As states develop public agendas for higher education they should incorporate the perspectives of not only those within colleges and universities but also those from outside the academy, such as political, business, and community leaders. These discussions can be useful teaching moments from both sides (inside and outside higher education); faculty often do not understand the assumptions of the business community at the same time that community, political, and business leaders often misunderstand purely academic policies such as promotion and tenure. A clearer understanding by all involved allows for a better policy foundation to be built for future expansion. Comparative policy analysts should attempt to incorporate multiple perspectives—academic, business, political, and average citizen—into their work.

Recommending Policy Changes

The final activity in the development of a public agenda for higher education is to recommend policy changes, policy additions, and implementation steps. At this stage it is important to assign responsibilities, as appropriate, to the key actors—executive branch, legislature, higher education agencies, and institutions. It is important to have—and implement—a strategy for building shared understanding about the public agenda beyond the leadership group. It is critically important that the message be delivered in a consistent way. The same data and the same description of the state must be heard by all involved, so that the rationale for the public agenda is transparent. Here involvement of all stakeholder groups, including the media, is important. An example of a succinct and consistent message is illustrated by the five questions that the state of Kentucky developed to guide the implementation of new higher education policy:

1. Are more Kentuckians ready for postsecondary education?
2. Are more students enrolling?

3. Are more students advancing?
4. Are we preparing Kentuckians?
5. Is Kentucky benefiting?

Kentucky arrived at these questions after moving through (albeit in a nonlinear fashion) the various steps to developing a public agenda for higher education as described in this chapter. These simple questions provide focal points for policy discussions and for accountability and a "handle" the media can use in discussing higher education in the commonwealth.

The final lesson to inform comparative-state higher education policy work is to be aware of recommended policies and how they will be implemented. Despite best efforts, existing and new policies could be particularly synergistic or antagonistic, and that interplay will affect any policy comparison.

Conclusion

As I have illustrated, a multitude of methodological issues occur when working with states on developing public agendas for higher education that provide some important lessons for those doing comparative-state higher education policy work. Many of these issues have to do with data and can be addressed through specific and clear explanation. But, additional problems can arise when others either disallow the use of satisficing and estimation or when data used in estimation is presented as definitive data rather than as an estimation tool to continue to move the conversation forward.

Through work with the Collaborative states and others engaged in similar processes, the participating organizations have become convinced that the approach described in this chapter constitutes an effective means of developing and implementing a change agenda for state higher education policy. Through the four-step process—collecting and analyzing existing data, engaging a broad range of stakeholders in examining the results of data analysis, conducting a policy audit, and developing an action plan—agreement on priorities can be forged, policy barriers uncovered, needs for new policies identified, and implementation strategies designed with responsibilities for various parts of the strategies assigned to the appropriate entities.

Yet researchers comparing or participating in higher education policy agenda setting across states need to be aware of the multiple ways in which states differ. These differences, which include historical, political, financial, and structural factors, will have a strong effect on how the Collaborative's model will be implemented. Nevertheless, although states are truly different, they all share a common goal: to meet the needs of their citizens and thrive as communities in a global economy.

References

Carnevale, A. P., & Desrochers, D. M. (2003). *Standards for what? The economic roots of K–16 reform*. Princeton, NJ: Educational Testing Service.

Davies, G. K. (2004). The next ten years: Not business as usual. *Continuing Higher Education Review, 68*, 29–36.

Kelly, P. J., & Jones, D. P. (2005, December). *A new look at the institutional component of higher education finance: A guide for evaluating performance relative to financial resources*. Boulder, CO: National Center for Higher Education Management Systems. [Available at: www.higheredinfo.org/analy ses/Policy%20Guide%20Dec2005.pdf].

Kingdon, J. W. (1995). *Agendas, alternatives, and public policies* (2nd ed.). New York: Longman.

National Center for Higher Education Management Systems. (2003, May). *Conceptualizing and researching the educational pipeline*. NCHEMS News, Volume 20. Boulder, CO: Author. [Available at: www.nchems.org/News/ NCHEMS%20News%20May2003.pdf].

National Center for Higher Education Management Systems. (2005, October). *Frequently asked questions about the educational pipeline*. Boulder, CO: Author. [Available at: www.higheredinfo.org/analyses/Pipeline_FAQ.pdf].

Rainwater, T. (2005, June/July). Increasing educational opportunities: Improving state policy to offer higher education to all. *State News, 48*(6), 25–28. [Available at: www.csg.org/pubs/Documents/sn0507.pdf].

Simon, H. A. (1976). *Administrative behavior: A study of decision-making processes in administrative organization* (3rd ed.). New York: The Free Press.

Contributors

Thomas Bailey is the George and Abby O'Neill Professor of Economics and Education in the Department of International and Transcultural Studies at Teachers College, Columbia University. Dr. Bailey holds a Ph.D. in labor economics from MIT and is an expert on the economics of education, educational policy, community colleges, and the educational and training implications of changes in the workplace. He is the director of the Community College Research Center and the Institute on Education and the Economy. He is also director of the newly established National Center for Research on Postsecondary Education, funded by the U.S. Department of Education.

Jennifer A. Delaney is an advanced doctoral student in the higher education program at Stanford University. She has worked as a policy analyst with the National Center for Public Policy and Higher Education where she contributed to *Measuring Up 2004* and served as a consultant for the Secretary of Education's Commission on the Future of Higher Education. Previously she held the position of assistant staff director for research with the Advisory Committee on Student Financial Assistance. She holds a masters degree in higher education from Harvard University and a Bachelor of Arts degree in English from the University of Michigan.

William R. Doyle is assistant professor of higher education in the Department of Leadership, Policy and Organizations at Peabody College of Vanderbilt University. He holds a Ph.D. in higher education from Stanford University. Prior to coming to Vanderbilt, he held the position of senior policy analyst at the National Center for Public Policy and Higher Education.

Sara Goldrick-Rab is assistant professor of educational policy studies and sociology at the University of Wisconsin–Madison and affiliate of the Wisconsin Center for the Advancement of Postsecondary Education and the Consortium for Chicago School Research. She was named a Rising Scholar by the National Forum on Higher Education for the Public Good

(2004) and is an NAE/Spencer Foundation postdoctoral fellow (2006–2007). Her research on inequality in postsecondary transitions is published in *Sociology of Education, Educational Evaluation and Policy Analysis*, and *Teachers College Record*, and she is the coauthor of *Putting Poor People to Work*, published by Russell Sage in 2006.

James C. Hearn is professor of higher education at the University of Georgia's Institute of Higher Education. Professor Hearn's research and teaching focus on postsecondary education policy and organization. In recent work, he has investigated 1) state and federal policies directed toward financing student access, choice, and persistence in postsecondary education, 2) state and federal policies affecting governance and decision making in postsecondary institutions, and 3) trends toward marketization in postsecondary-education policy, governance, finance, and management. Professor Hearn's research has been published in sociology, economics, and education journals as well as in several books. He serves on the editorial boards of *Teachers College Record*, the *Review of Higher Education*, and the Vanderbilt University Press and is associate editor of *Research in Higher Education*. He holds a Ph.D. in the sociology of education and an M.A. in sociology from Stanford University.

Donald E. Heller is associate professor and senior research associate at the Center for the Study of Higher Education at Pennsylvania State University. His research centers on higher education economics, public policy, and finance and college access and choice. He earned Ed.M. and Ed.D. degrees from the Harvard Graduate School of Education, and a B.A. in Economics and Political Science from Tufts University. He is the editor of the books *The States and Public Higher Education Policy: Affordability, Access, and Accountability* (Johns Hopkins University Press, 2001), and *Condition of Access: Higher Education for Lower Income Students* (ACE/Praeger, 2002).

Michael K. McLendon is associate professor of public policy and higher education and director of the Program in Higher Education Leadership and Policy at Peabody College of Vanderbilt University. His research focuses on the role of political institutions and postsecondary governance structures in shaping state policy outcomes for higher education. His recent projects include studies of the determinants of tuition and appropriations patterns in public higher education and the origins and spread of performance-accountability mandates for higher education. Dr. McLendon's research has appeared in *The Journal of Higher Education, Educational Evaluation and Policy Analysis, Higher Education: Handbook of*

Theory and Research, Educational Policy, Research in Higher Education, and *Review of Higher Education.* He serves as associate editor for *Higher Education: Handbook of Theory and Research* and *Research in Higher Education.* He holds a Ph.D. in higher education from the University of Michigan.

Karen Paulson is a senior associate at the National Center for Higher Education Management Systems (NCHEMS). Her areas of expertise include assessment, evaluation, and the use of data in state policymaking. Currently she is evaluating state activities for the State Scholars Initiative, a program administered by WICHE for the federal Office of Vocational and Adult Education. She is the author of *Adult Learners in the United States: A National Profile* (coauthored with Marianne Boeke for the American Council on Education, 2006), *A Data Audit and Analysis Toolkit to Support Assessment of the First College Year* (2003), and *Following the Mobile Student: Can We Develop the Capacity for a Comprehensive Database to Assess Student Progression?* (coauthored with Peter Ewell and Paula Schild for the Lumina Foundation for Education Research Report, 2003). She holds engineering degrees in addition to her higher education study. Her Ph.D. is in higher education with a minor in policy analysis from The Pennsylvania State University.

Kathleen M. Shaw is associate professor of urban education at Temple University. She is currently on leave from Temple to serve as Deputy Secretary for Postsecondary and Higher Education in Pennsylvania. Her scholarship focuses on issues of access and equity in higher education, with a particular emphasis on how large-scale federal and state policy affects higher education policy and practice. Her work has been supported by the Lumina Foundation, the Russell Sage Foundation, the Spencer Foundation, the Annie E. Casey Foundation, and Atlantic Philanthropies. Her book *Putting Poor People to Work: How the Work-First Idea Eroded College Access for the Poor* (coauthored with Sara Goldrick-Rab, Jerry A. Jacobs, and Christopher Mazzeo) was published in 2006 by the Russell Sage Foundation Press.

INDEX